The Art of Losing

The Art of Losing

POEMS OF GRIEF AND HEALING

EDITED BY

Kevin Young

NEW YORK   BERLIN   LONDON

Published by Bloomsbury USA, New York

All papers used by Bloomsbury USA are natural, recyclable products made from wood grown in well-managed forests. The manufacturing processes conform to the environmental regulations of the country of origin.

LIBRARY OF CONGRESS CATALOGING-IN-PUBLICATION DATA

Young, Kevin.
The art of losing : poems of grief and healing / Kevin Young.—1st U.S. ed.
p. cm.
ISBN 978-1-60819-033-1
1. Grief—Poetry. I. Title.
PS3575.O798A89 2010
811'.54—dc22
2009028888

First U.S. Edition 2010

1   3   5   7   9   10   8   6   4   2

Interior design by Sara E. Stemen
Typeset by Westchester Book Group
Printed in the United States of America by Worldcolor Fairfield

For my father

O how shall I warble myself for the dead one there I loved?
And how shall I deck my song for the large sweet soul that has gone?

—WALT WHITMAN

CONTENTS

II. Regret

I believe, but what is belief?

III. Remembrance *What did I know, what did I know . . .*

IV. Ritual

Tomorrow, the bowl I have yet to fill.

V. Recovery

I learn by going where I have to go.

VI. Redemption   *What will survive of us is love.*

INTRODUCTION

I have begun to believe in, and even to preach, a poetry of necessity. This is a recognition not just of the necessity of poetry to our lives, but also the fact that necessity is what drives most of the poetry that matters, or the way that it matters. The best poems, it seems to me, evince their origins in the need to speak, or to write; to render a complex fate simply; to render chaos as chaos; or to examine the unseen complexities of seemingly simple, even everyday, experience. A poem must be willing to be unwilled, beckoned by need.

No one wants to write an elegy. I presume we simply must, the death of someone dear—or even a stranger—calling forth words that fail to explain, but sometimes provide our only comfort. It is out of such need, and for its consolation, that I have gathered the poems in this anthology: to reveal the many ways poets seek to find words and form to contain loss; and to fulfill the reader's need for comfort and companionship in the words of another. Often, in death, everything else fails. We are left only with the music and the meaning of poetry.

The Art of Losing gathers together some of the best contemporary elegies—mainly those written in the twentieth century and after—with a particular focus on recent poems. I have included one or two nineteenth-century poems that seem to me absolutely necessary and remarkably modern—as with the powerful work of Emily Dickinson and the "[Carrion Comfort]" of Gerard Manley Hopkins—but have for the most part tried to stick to poems that are contemporary classics, or soon ought to be. The poems here focus on grief and its healing, however tentative or untold.

Truth be known, I was surprised not to find this book already on bookstore shelves. There have been a few academic studies of the history of the elegy, and a few collections of poems about mourning, featuring some of the more familiar lines—John Donne's "Death be not proud," for instance—that may come to mind when someone dies. But it seemed time to engage our current day's perspective on loss, which, while it draws on a long history of understanding bereavement, also attempts to interpret it anew. Indeed, one key aspect of contemporary elegy is the desire to represent the experience, to re-experience it through language—to evoke, that is, and not just describe, the pain of passing. In doing so, these poems focus less on the often formal process of mourning and instead on the personal and often bewildering process of grief.

In a way, the process of grief, I have found, can mirror that of writing: it is surprising, trying, frustrating, daunting, terrifying, comforting, chastening, challenging, and at times, heartening; grief can provide fellowship with others interested in the experience; it brings out the best in us, and at times the worst, if only because it is utterly human. It can feel inevitable, but it is so personal, so differently pitched for each, that it can reside across a great gulf. Yet poetry, like grief, can be the thing that bridges the gap between us, that brings us together and binds us.

The music of the modern elegy has no set form. It can be short or long; a well-wrought outpouring like Donald Hall's "Without"; or an almost mute rendering of the stunned shock of loss, like Brenda Shaughnessy's "Ever." Modern elegy encompasses the formal restraint of W. H. Auden's "Funeral Blues"—its tight rhyme, like that of the blues form, fighting the *feeling* of being blue—and the stark emotional restraint of Emily Dickinson's "After great pain, a formal feeling comes—." This "formal feeling" of mourning recognizes that public mourning, with its rituals and rites, can often rescue us from overwhelming feeling. Such traditions provide their own comfort, and the elegy's long tradition— its feeling in form—proves no different.

Yet elegies are not ideas. They are experiences, carved out of our individual perspective and our collective journey through this life. It is tempting to say this is true as well of most good poems, but that might be overstating it—there are, after all, many significant and even moving poems about thinking, about the meditative parts of human nature. When it comes to grief, however, thinking alone is no good. To lose someone close to you is to enter an experience no amount of forethought or hindsight can free you from. You must live through grief. You cannot outsmart it, nor think through the fact of someone's being gone, and forever. You must survive the sorrow. This does not mean that the elegy cannot contemplate; indeed, with luck, one emerges from grief not just with emptiness, but wisdom—though of a kind you'd gladly unlearn for your loved one to return.

After my father suddenly died, killed in an accident, I would have given near anything to have him return to us, even for just a moment. Instead, I waited for him to visit me, in dream if that's what was meant to be. He never did. I realize now that such visitations, as Natasha Trethewey's poem "Myth" enacts, bring their own sorrows—the stark light of morning reinforcing the ongoing mourning—despite dream's temporary reprieve.

> I was asleep while you were dying.
> It's as if you slipped through some rift, a hollow
> I make between my slumber and my waking,
>
> the Erebus I keep you in, still trying
> not to let go. You'll be dead again tomorrow,
> but in dreams you live. So I try taking
>
> you back into morning. Sleep-heavy, turning,
> my eyes open, I find you do not follow.
> Again and again, this constant forsaking.

What grief tells us is that you don't always get a chance to say good-bye. And yet in many ways, the poetic elegy does just that. Sometimes it says *So long*; sometimes *See you 'round*; sometimes the poem's filled with anger, asking *Why?*; other poems say simply, *Wait*. Galway Kinnell's poem of that name, "Wait"—an entreaty for someone to stay in this world, not to leave too early—can also be read as a desire to console the living about the experience of loss:

> Wait, for now.
> Distrust everything if you have to.
> But trust the hours. Haven't they
> carried you everywhere, up to now?
> Personal events will become interesting again.
> Hair will become interesting.
> Pain will become interesting.
> Buds that open out of season will become interesting.
> Second-hand gloves will become lovely again;
> their memories are what give them
> the need for other hands.

Though dedicated to the dead, in a crucial way elegies are written for the living. Honoring the departed, these poems connect with the idea of loss in a way that may comfort those left behind, if only as companions in grief.

To lose someone today is to go into strange realms of "bereavement specialists" and sympathy cards and funeral arrangements—things you suddenly realize have been going on for a good while, without you, in something of a parallel world. The world of grief can feel like that, a limbo realm that at the least gives you a strong perspective on the everyday world: Why are all these people walking around, oblivious to loss? Why am I still here while my loved one is not? Surviving any death can carry its own guilt. It also brings on a slew of clichés, often offered in lieu of sympathy, that can sometimes cause more anxiety than comfort. It is hard to know what to say. The poems here seek to avoid cliché, in order to say what needs to be said. And also to say that it is the everyday, not the epic; the unexpected, not the well-worn phrase that the modern elegy may find most comforting.

In my own grief it was and is the smallest kindnesses that still stick with me: the man who gave me my father's dry cleaning for free, refusing my repeated offers to pay; the dry cleaning I'd had to drive all over town looking for, using old tags found on other of his still-plastic-wrapped clothes as a guide. How to explain "I'm looking for my dead father's clothes, things he'll never need," yet that, duty-bound, you do? Death brings with it a duty and devotion that cannot be explained to those who don't know it. Why, after all, would you keep his crummy plaid shirts and give his good suits away? Why do material things matter at once less and more? Why, in the void, does ritual, both inherited and invented, rush in?

The poems in this collection consider less than this, and more: duty, hindsight, sorrow, fury, frustration, acceptance, even transcendence. I have structured the book something like the journey of mourning—not the now-classic stages of grief (as laid out by Elisabeth Kübler-Ross in her groundbreaking *On Death and Dying*), but something more like the range of responses to it. And if in its movement from Reckoning to Regret, through Remembrance to Ritual and Recovery, this book doesn't necessarily resolve the grieving process with simple acceptance, it does end with a kind of Redemption, much as in Kinnell: *Hair will become interesting.* And with it, life. The countless little details that make life up—that in the throes of grief seem at once unbearable and meaningless—may become interesting again.

These details are expressed in every section of the book. Reckoning, the book's first section, encompasses the immediate reactions to a death, whether long expected or sudden—an experience where the world is both more present, and far less. "Stop all the clocks," "Do not pick up the telephone," "Do not go gentle into that good night," "Let evening come": no wonder the voice here is often imperative, still reeling, arguing, and even denying as it takes comfort where it can.

Reckoning gives way to Regret, a section where wishes meet memory, from one last look to "forgiving my father." The third section, Remembrance, further considers the relationship to memory—for memory is grief's parent and its offspring. If Reckoning is filled with orders to "Let evening come" or resist going gently into the dark, then Remembrance is often filled with questioning as well as comfort: *What did I know, what did I know/Of Love's austere and lonely offices?* That is, grief spawns memories of the departed, which, in turn, can spawn more grief—but just as often these memories are a balm to mourners, who gather and recollect, who tell tales and perhaps even laugh about those missed.

Such gathering is at the heart of this anthology and also of its fourth section, Ritual, which considers both the public and private sides of the various rites of mourning—from cleaning out a loved one's closet, to pallbearing, to prayer or its attempt, to refashioning a new set of traditions, to sharing the memory of the departed in conversation or over a last meal. Memory may indeed be like the food found after a wake, whether in the African American tradition of repast or the feasts that follow many a memorial service. This breaking bread afterward is a form of ceremony every bit as crucial as the service itself. Remembrance and the rituals of mourning sustain us individually even as they bring us together.

I am struck here that in our times of need, or high celebration, we reach for poetry just as we do food. It seems that the music of poetry—whether a love poem for a wedding or a verse of whatever holy book we believe in—helps us mark an occasion, to recognize its importance, and even to help set it apart. While this might seem to relegate poetry to mere monument, I think it is in grief that we need some reminder of our humanity—and, sometimes, someone to say it for us. Poetry steps in at those moments when ordinary words fail: poetry as ceremony, as closure to what cannot be closed.

Even healing hurts. Ritual may eventually give way to Recovery, the title of the fifth section of the book—recovery not being something inevitable, but something that can surprise us survivors, what Jane Mayhall calls "this complex, heartbreak survival." One need not be a poet like W. S. Merwin to experience the shock of finding oneself "in life as in a strange garment"—but we may need his description of it. Like all elegies, in some key way this section is for the living, who may go on to seek the kind of Redemption found in the last section of the book, which opens with Philip Larkin's "The Trees":

> The trees are coming into leaf
> Like something almost being said;
> The recent buds relax and spread,
> Their greenness is a kind of grief.

The greenness of grief—its returning, like the leaves—seems to me one of the best ways to understand it as an experience. It is perennial, yet ebbs and flows, "Like something almost being said." Even grief's lessening can be something to be mourned; ironically, there are days when, by not feeling so bad, we fear and feel we are betraying our loved ones.

This attempt to remember, speak of, argue with, and honor the dead is exactly what the elegies in this volume chart. Full of forms and full of fury, these poems are reconciled and inconsolable, ragged and raw and filled with revelation. This book's title comes from a poem that itself is about trying to cope with loss, Elizabeth Bishop's "One Art," with its famous last lines:

> It's evident
> the art of losing's not too hard to master
> though it may look like (*Write* it!) like disaster.

This convincing of the self, a self-conscious mustering of courage, is one thing that may separate the modern elegy from those that went before, though most elegies seem to require an appeal to someone, or something, some force of nature greater than the self in order to help say the words being written. Elegies often get their power from declaring they have none.

You may have already noted that Bishop's "One Art" is not

technically an elegy—at least, its impetus is not strictly speaking a death, but the end of a relationship. (And more.) Yet the "loss" discussed by Bishop, if not a literal death, seems in the poem a symbolic one. So I have decided to include it.

The thing about death is: it isn't symbolic, but very real. Yet in our elegiac age, the tone of elegy, however varied, has been borrowed to discuss everything from lost childhoods to the loss of childhood friends. Apart from one or two instances, I have resisted too broad a definition—I have generally not included poems, say, of illness or other difficulties or life passages, simply because there seems nothing quite like bereavement itself. And yet on a few occasions, such as "One Art" or Joseph Brodsky's "A Song," when a poem seems somehow to transform in the light of loss, where missing the Beloved can be read in a way that sheds light on the Departed, I have included it.

I have chosen, I should note, not to include one of the strongest strains of elegy: the poem mourning or celebrating a famous person or literary or popular figure after his or her passing. This is the source of many of our most powerful elegies, from poems about jazz musicians to those dedicated to fellow poets—often people who weren't mere icons to those writing the poems, but friends and loved ones. Especially as I have previously included some of these in my *Blues Poems* and *Jazz Poems* anthologies, I made a decision early on to focus here on the personal, rather than the iconic, side of elegy.

Working within such parameters we may miss out on W. H. Auden's beautiful "In Memory of W. B. Yeats," with its powerful descriptions and its claim that "poetry makes nothing happen"—a declaration that seems belied by the poem itself. Yet we gain Auden's "Funeral Blues," which I think is one of the heights of the form and which may indeed inaugurate the contemporary elegy. Its dispassionate testimony, its unerring grief, its blunt riffing off the musical form—which Auden seems to capture quite well, the strictness of his form substituting for the blues' repeating phrases and tragicomic humor—all seem part of the modern elegy. So too, Auden's "Musée des Beaux Arts," which describes everyday suffering in a way many readers have found redemptive in their own reading, painting as it does a view of how suffering often happens while we're not looking. Or worse, looking away, and on. One modern aspect of elegy is the way in which death seems our one certainty, and yet the one thing we cannot easily discuss. These poems seek to remedy this.

Since Auden's time, the contemporary elegy as represented here has allowed itself to be heartbroken, but also humorous; metaphoric, but also visceral; comforted and, as in Auden's own "Funeral Blues," beyond comforting. Sometimes an elegy does this all at once. The contemporary elegy offers testimony that both describes and defies what Auden speaks of in "Musée des Beaux Arts": "About suffering they were never wrong,/ The Old Masters." The new masters of the elegy here agree with the notion that the world goes on without noticing loss, even as their poems disprove it.

For my father's first funeral, in Kansas, where he died—before his subsequent burial and a second funeral in Louisiana, where he was born—I actually asked my earliest writing mentor to read "Funeral Blues." To some it may have seemed a bleak choice, but for me it represented one key side of grief: the shock, surprise, and short shrift one can feel upon hearing such news, as expressed in the book's Reckoning section:

> He was my North, my South, my East and West,
> My working week and my Sunday rest,
> My noon, my midnight, my talk, my song;
> I thought that love would last for ever: I was wrong.

I hadn't picked Auden arbitrarily, as he was a poet my father liked—indeed, the only poet I know of his buying. (With my books, he didn't have a choice, as I sent them to him!) Among his things, and the books and notes I sent him, several of which I didn't even remember sending, was an Auden volume he'd bought. In the front of the *Collected Poems* my father had copied out two lines:

If equal affection cannot be,
Let the more loving one be me.

It strikes me now that this one piece of poetry my father found moving enough to scrawl in his own hand might be said to speak to the mourner's wish: to love more, to continue loving even when one cannot hear from the beloved any longer. Indeed, it is too often that death clarifies a love that was there all along.

It is my sincere hope that these poems, the best of our time, may help us on our journey—not just in contemplating death, but in living our lives. They may remind us, as a source as seemingly unlikely as Philip Larkin does, that "we should be kind/While there is still time" and to "Begin afresh, afresh, afresh." Elegies are just as often for the living, remember. And while these poems chronicle loss and its rituals, elegies also celebrate life—and ask us to care for ours, if only by honoring others. And, in that way, "death shall have no dominion."

—KEVIN YOUNG
Belmont, Massachusetts

I.
Reckoning

Between grief and nothing, I will take grief.
—WILLIAM FAULKNER

Musée des Beaux Arts

W. H. AUDEN

About suffering they were never wrong,
The Old Masters: how well they understood
Its human position; how it takes place
While someone else is eating or opening a window or just walking
    dully along;
How, when the aged are reverently, passionately waiting
For the miraculous birth, there always must be
Children who did not specially want it to happen, skating
On a pond at the edge of the wood:
They never forgot
That even the dreadful martyrdom must run its course
Anyhow in a corner, some untidy spot
Where the dogs go on with their doggy life and the torturer's horse
Scratches its innocent behind on a tree.

In Brueghel's *Icarus*, for instance: how everything turns away
Quite leisurely from the disaster; the ploughman may
Have heard the splash, the forsaken cry,
But for him it was not an important failure; the sun shone
As it had to on the white legs disappearing into the green
Water; and the expensive delicate ship that must have seen
Something amazing, a boy falling out of the sky,
Had somewhere to get to and sailed calmly on.

Dying

ROBERT PINSKY

Nothing to be said about it, and everything—
The change of changes, closer or further away:
The Golden Retriever next door, Gussie, is dead,

Like Sandy, the Cocker Spaniel from three doors down
Who died when I was small; and every day
Things that were in my memory fade and die.

Phrases die out: first, everyone forgets
What doornails are; then after certain decades
As a dead metaphor, "*dead as a doornail*" flickers

And fades away. But someone I know is dying—
And though one might say glibly, "everyone is,"
The different pace makes the difference absolute.

The tiny invisible spores in the air we breathe,
That settle harmlessly on our drinking water
And on our skin, happen to come together

With certain conditions on the forest floor,
Or even a shady corner of the lawn—
And overnight the fleshy, pale stalks gather,

The colorless growth without a leaf or flower;
And around the stalks, the summer grass keeps growing
With steady pressure, like the insistent whiskers

That grow between shaves on a face, the nails
Growing and dying from the toes and fingers
At their own humble pace, oblivious

As the nerveless moths, that live their night or two—
Though like a moth a bright soul keeps on beating,
Bored and impatient in the monster's mouth.

The Wake

RITA DOVE

Your absence distributed itself
like an invitation.
Friends and relatives
kept coming, trying
to fill up the house.
But the rooms still gaped—
the green hanger swang empty, and
the head of the table
demanded a plate.

When I sat down in the armchair
your warm breath fell
over my shoulder.
When I climbed to bed I walked
through your blind departure.
The others stayed downstairs,
trying to cover
the silence with weeping.

When I lay down between the sheets
I lay down in the cool waters
of my own womb
and became the child
inside, innocuous
as a button, helplessly growing.
I slept because it was the only
thing I could do. I even dreamed.
I couldn't stop myself.

"After great pain, a formal feeling comes—"

EMILY DICKINSON

After great pain, a formal feeling comes—
The Nerves sit ceremonious, like Tombs—
The stiff Heart questions was it He, that bore,
And Yesterday, or Centuries before?

The Feet, mechanical, go round—
Of Ground, or Air, or Ought—
A Wooden way
Regardless grown,
A Quartz contentment, like a stone—

This is the Hour of Lead—
Remembered, if outlived,
As Freezing persons, recollect the Snow—
First—Chill—then Stupor—then the letting go—

"My life closed twice before its close—"

EMILY DICKINSON

My life closed twice before its close—
It yet remains to see
If Immortality unveil
A third event to me

So huge, so hopeless to conceive
As these that twice befell.
Parting is all we know of heaven,
And all we need of hell.

Secret Knowledge

BRENDA HILLMAN

At first I was able to speak to her quickly
just by closing my eyes.

She had died in the first week of quinces,
when things put forth their secret knowledge:
fiery, random blossoms are allowed to live,

and robins don't seem all that common
as they swing at the tops of cypresses
through new song;

and I wanted to hear just one voice
but I heard two,
wanted to be just one thing, but I was several;

I called her more quickly,
told her how much I missed her,
pausing at the edge of the screen

that kept me from her
in all the awkwardness of living,

and she said it was not up to me
to live without her
or make the voice be single,

she said every voice is needed.
Every voice cries out in its own way—

Much Hurrying

BRENDA HILLMAN

—So much hurrying right after a death:
as if a bride were waiting!

Crocuses sliced themselves out
with their penknives. Everything well made
seemed dead to them: Camelias. Their butcher-
paper pink. The well-made poems
seemed dead to you,

only what was vastly overheard would do,

you had to say something so general
over the edge
that everyone could hear—the guests,
the bride—though the edge
was specific to you, the edge was inside—

The Race

SHARON OLDS

When I got to the airport I rushed up to the desk,
bought a ticket, ten minutes later
they told me the flight was cancelled, the doctors
had said my father would not live through the night
and the flight was cancelled. A young man
with a dark brown moustache told me
another airline had a nonstop
leaving in seven minutes. See that
elevator over there, well go
down to the first floor, make a right, you'll
see a yellow bus, get off at the
second Pan Am terminal, I
ran, I who have no sense of direction
raced exactly where he'd told me, a fish
slipping upstream deftly against
the flow of the river. I jumped off that bus with those
bags I had thrown everything into
in five minutes, and ran, the bags
wagged me from side to side as if
to prove I was under the claims of the material,
I ran up to a man with a flower on his breast,
I who always go to the end of the line, I said
Help me. He looked at my ticket, he said
Make a left and then a right, go up the moving stairs and then
run. I lumbered up the moving stairs,
at the top I saw the corridor,
and then I took a deep breath, I said
Goodbye to my body, goodbye to comfort,

I used my legs and heart as if I would
gladly use them up for this,
to touch him again in this life. I ran, and the
bags banged against me, wheeled and coursed
in skewed orbits, I have seen pictures of
women running, their belongings tied
in scarves grasped in their fists, I blessed my
long legs he gave me, my strong
heart I abandoned to its own purpose,
I ran to Gate 17 and they were
just lifting the thick white
lozenge of the door to fit it into
the socket of the plane. Like the one who is not
too rich, I turned sideways and
slipped through the needle's eye, and then
I walked down the aisle toward my father. The jet
was full, and people's hair was shining, they were
smiling, the interior of the plane was filled with a
mist of gold endorphin light,
I wept as people weep when they enter heaven,
in massive relief. We lifted up
gently from one tip of the continent
and did not stop until we set down lightly on the
other edge, I walked into his room
and watched his chest rise slowly
and sink again, all night
I watched him breathe.

The Whale

TERRANCE HAYES

for Purvis

Just like that your father's dead,
Half of all the footsteps you've made

In your lifetime swept away by the tide
Gnawing the shore, the bits of shells
Like fragments of bone and teeth sinking

Into the sand beneath you as you walk
Toward the people crowding the body

Of a young whale, a boy on the shoulders
Of his father, a woman slipping film into a camera,
The skin peeling on a lifeguard's neck

As he stoops peering into the animal's eye,
Saying nothing, the audience silent or silenced

By the sound of saltwater sweet-talking the shore
As if sweet-talking the earth from her prom dress,
The tide stroking its hands along her inner thigh

And finding the crop of razor bumps
Like the humped tiny backs of shells

And smiling at the thought of the girl preparing
For her prom date, the hair lathered
And shaved away, the air leaving ripples inside

The dress as the knee-high hem is lifted
Above the girl's waist and breasts,

The sound of the silk passing over her body
Like the sound of the tide uncovering
And then covering the hard news of the day,

The news returning each time it's washed away.

Silence

D. H. LAWRENCE

Since I lost you, I am silence-haunted;
   Sounds wave their little wings
A moment, then in weariness settle
   On the flood that soundless swings.

Whether the people in the street
   Like pattering-ripples go by,
Or whether the theatre sighs and sighs
   With a loud, hoarse sigh:

Or the wind shakes a ravel of light
   Over the dead-black river,
Or last night's echoings
   Make the daybreak shiver:

I feel the silence waiting
   To sip them all up again,
In its last completeness drinking
   Down the noise of men.

Futility

WILFRED OWEN

Move him into the sun—
Gently its touch awoke him once,
At home, whispering of fields unsown.
Always it woke him, even in France,
Until this morning and this snow.
If anything might rouse him now
The kind old sun will know.

Think how it wakes the seeds,—
Woke, once, the clays of a cold star.
Are limbs, so dear-achieved, are sides,
Full-nerved—still warm—too hard to stir?
Was it for this the clay grew tall?
—O what made fatuous sunbeams toil
To break earth's sleep at all?

Lament

ANNE SEXTON

Someone is dead.
Even the trees know it,
those poor old dancers who come on lewdly,
all pea-green scarfs and spine pole.
I think . . .
I think I could have stopped it,
if I'd been as firm as a nurse
or noticed the neck of the driver
as he cheated the crosstown lights;
or later in the evening,
if I'd held my napkin over my mouth.
I think I could . . .
if I'd been different, or wise, or calm,
I think I could have charmed the table,
the stained dish or the hand of the dealer.
But it's done.
It's all used up.
There's no doubt about the trees
spreading their thin feet into the dry grass.
A Canada goose rides up,
spread out like a gray suede shirt,
honking his nose into the March wind.
In the entryway a cat breathes calmly
into her watery blue fur.
The supper dishes are over and the sun
unaccustomed to anything else
goes all the way down.

Not Waving But Drowning

STEVIE SMITH

Nobody heard him, the dead man,
But still he lay moaning:
I was much further out than you thought
And not waving but drowning.

Poor chap, he always loved larking
And now he's dead
It must have been too cold for him his heart gave way,
They said.

Oh, no no no, it was too cold always
(Still the dead one lay moaning)
I was much too far out all my life
And not waving but drowning.

Do Not Go Gentle into That Good Night

DYLAN THOMAS

Do not go gentle into that good night,
Old age should burn and rave at close of day;
Rage, rage against the dying of the light.

Though wise men at their end know dark is right,
Because their words had forked no lightning they
Do not go gentle into that good night.

Good men, the last wave by, crying how bright
Their frail deeds might have danced in a green bay,
Rage, rage against the dying of the light.

Wild men who caught and sang the sun in flight,
And learn, too late, they grieved it on its way,
Do not go gentle into that good night.

Grave men, near death, who see with blinding sight
Blind eyes could blaze like meteors and be gay,
Rage, rage against the dying of the light.

And you, my father, there on the sad height,
Curse, bless, me now with your fierce tears, I pray.
Do not go gentle into that good night.
Rage, rage against the dying of the light.

Pyrrhic Victory

LUCIE BROCK-BROIDO

When you have won, good voyager, your pilgrimage will be
Calamitous as a victory

Got by slashing and burning your own tailored fields of gold.

A cocoon will bloom in the empty chest of the beloved, lavishly.

I do not want to be a chrysalis again.
How long will I have to live here quickened in

My finespun case, like a folded pilgrim, blushing,
Till I am moth.

The nightmares have come back
Like women winding their hair in sullen braids, untroubling

As the sound of flour being sifted onto parchment, shifting
As it winnows itself.

Powder is dread, refined.
The imperative: to win.

And all this happened after keeping mute for many years

Like a sallow box of baking soda with no expiration date,

Innocuous, absorbing everything.
Some grief is larger than my body is.

The Mower

PHILIP LARKIN

The mower stalled, twice; kneeling, I found
A hedgehog jammed up against the blades,
Killed. It had been in the long grass.

I had seen it before, and even fed it, once.
Now I had mauled its unobtrusive world
Unmendably. Burial was no help:

Next morning I got up and it did not.
The first day after a death, the new absence
Is always the same; we should be careful

Of each other, we should be kind
While there is still time.

No More

MARY JO BANG

Goodbye to forever now.
Hello to the empty present and.
Goodbye to the orchids woven
With something that looks like a seed weed.

Hello to the day
We looked out through
The juniper smudge
Burned to remember the moment.

The doctoring moment is over.
A sheaf of paper drops like lead
From the tree of the table it came from.
The eyes play tricks.

The quilt edge clasped in the hand
Goes on and on and on.
Rumination is this. You
A child, then a man, now a feather

Passing through a furious fire
Called time. The cone of some plant
From a place I don't know
In the high flames.

Rumination is and won't stop
With the stoppered bottle, the pills
On the floor, the broken plate
On the floor, the sleeping face

In the bassinette of your birth month,
The dog bite, the difficulty,
The stairwell of a three-flat
Of your sixth year, the flood

Of farthering off this all takes you
As thought and object become
What you are. My stoppered mind.
A voice, carried by machine,

Across a lifeless body. Across
A lacerating lapse in time.

Loss

RUTH STONE

I hid sometimes in the closet among my own clothes.
It was no use. The pain would wake me
Or like a needle it would stitch its way into my dreams.
Whenever I turned
I saw its eyes looking out of the eyes of strangers.
In the night I would walk from room to room slowly
Like an old person in a convalescent home.
I would stare at the cornices, the dull arrangements of furniture.
It all remained the same.
It was not even a painting.
It was objects in space without any aura. No meaning attached.
Their very existence was a burden to me.
And I would go back to my bed whimpering.

Ever

BRENDA SHAUGHNESSY

Where, swift and wool in going?
Fell always wishing like this.

Tomorrow, want less and hunger bigger.
Fewer terror but stronger, staggered.

Taken heart outside to dry.
Rain surprise and ruined.

Silver cold and stops the swelling.
Why hurts from other body?

Why photo soothes with flat?
Salt soaks blood tender.

Brighten flesh in slap.
With word, not flood silent.

Not leave and take me
nowhere, swift and wool in going.

Sudden

NICK FLYNN

If it had been a heart attack, the newspaper
might have used the word *massive*,
      as if a mountain range had opened
         inside her, but instead

it used the word *suddenly*, a light coming on

in an empty room. The telephone

fell from my shoulder, a black parrot repeating
        something happened, something awful

    a sunday, dusky. If it had been

terminal, we could have cradled her
as she grew smaller, wiped her mouth,

     said good-bye. But it was *sudden*,

how overnight we could be orphaned
& the world become a bell we'd crawl inside
& the ringing all we'd eat.

Do Not Pick Up the Telephone

TED HUGHES

That plastic Buddha jars out a Karate screech

Before the soft words with their spores
The cosmetic breath of the gravestone

Death invented the phone it looks like the altar of death
Do not worship the telephone
It drags its worshippers into actual graves
With a variety of devices, through a variety of disguised voices

Sit godless when you hear the religious wail of the telephone

Do not think your house is a hide-out it is a telephone
Do not think you walk your own road, you walk down a telephone
Do not think you sleep in the hand of God you sleep in the
          mouthpiece of a telephone
Do not think your future is yours it waits upon a telephone
Do not think your thoughts are your own thoughts they are the
          toys of the telephone
Do not think these days are days they are the sacrificial priests
          of the telephone
The secret police of the telephone

O phone get out of my house
You are a bad god
Go and whisper on some other pillow
Do not lift your snake head in my house
Do not bite any more beautiful people

You plastic crab
Why is your oracle always the same in the end?
What rake-off for you from the cemeteries?

Your silences are as bad
When you are needed, dumb with the malice of the clairvoyant
            insane
The stars whisper together in your breathing
World's emptiness oceans in your mouthpiece
Stupidly your string dangles into the abysses
Plastic you are then stone a broken box of letters
And you cannot utter
Lies or truth, only the evil one
Makes you tremble with sudden appetite to see somebody undone

Blackening electrical connections
To where death bleaches its crystals
You swell and you writhe
You open your Buddha gape
You screech at the root of the house

Do not pick up the detonator of the telephone
A flame from the last day will come lashing out of the telephone
A dead body will fall out of the telephone

Do not pick up the telephone

Funeral Blues

W. H. AUDEN

Stop all the clocks, cut off the telephone,
Prevent the dog from barking with a juicy bone,
Silence the pianos and with muffled drum
Bring out the coffin, let the mourners come.

Let aeroplanes circle moaning overhead
Scribbling on the sky the message He is Dead,
Put crêpe bows round the white necks of the public doves,
Let the traffic policemen wear black cotton gloves.

He was my North, my South, my East and West,
My working week and my Sunday rest,
My noon, my midnight, my talk, my song;
I thought that love would last for ever: I was wrong.

The stars are not wanted now: put out every one;
Pack up the moon and dismantle the sun;
Pour away the ocean and sweep up the wood;
For nothing now can ever come to any good.

Graveyard Blues

NATASHA TRETHEWEY

It rained the whole time we were laying her down;
Rained from church to grave when we put her down.
The suck of mud at our feet was a hollow sound.

When the preacher called out I held up my hand;
When he called for a witness I raised my hand—
Death stops the body's work, the soul's a journeyman.

The sun came out when I turned to walk away,
Glared down on me as I turned and walked away—
My back to my mother, leaving her where she lay.

The road going home was pocked with holes,
That home-going road's always full of holes;
Though we slow down, time's wheel still rolls.

I wander now among names of the dead:
My mother's name, stone pillow for my head.

Without

DONALD HALL

we lived in a small island stone nation
without color under gray clouds and wind
distant the unlimited ocean acute
lymphoblastic leukemia without seagulls
or palm trees without vegetation
or animal life only barnacles and lead
colored moss that darkened when months did

hours days weeks months weeks days hours
the year endured without punctuation
february without ice winter sleet
snow melted recovered but nothing
without thaw although cold streams hurtled
no snowdrop or crocus rose no yellow
no red leaves of maple without october

no spring no summer no autumn no winter
no rain no peony thunder no woodthrush
the book was a thousand pages without commas
without mice oak leaves windstorms
no castles no plazas no flags no parrots
without carnival or the procession of relics
intolerable without brackets or colons

silence without color sound without smell
without apples without pork to rupture gnash
unpunctuated without churches uninterrupted
no orioles ginger noses no opera no
without fingers daffodils cheekbones

the body was a nation a tribe dug into stone
assaulted white blood broken to shards

provinces invaded bombed shot shelled
artillery sniper fire helicopter gunship
grenade burning murder landmine starvation
the ceasefire lasted forty-eight hours
then a shell exploded in a market
pain vomit neuropathy morphine nightmare
confusion the rack terror the vise

vincristine ara-c cytoxan vp-16
loss of memory loss of language losses
pneumocystis carinii pneumonia bactrim
foamless unmitigated sea without sea
delirium whipmarks of petechiae
multiple blisters of herpes zoster
and how are you doing today I am doing

one afternoon say the sun came out
moss took on greenishness leaves fell
the market opened a loaf of bread a sparrow
a bony dog wandered back sniffing a lath
it might be possible to take up a pencil
unwritten stanzas taken up and touched
beautiful terrible sentences unuttered

the sea unrelenting wave gray the sea
flotsam without islands broken crates
block after block the same house the mall
no cathedral no hobo jungle the same women
and men they longed to drink hayfields no
without dog or semicolon or village square
without monkey or lily without garlic

For a Woman Dead at Thirty

JEAN VALENTINE

No one ever talked like that before, like your
Last white rush in the still light of your
Last, bungled fever: no one will any more.

Now we breathe easier: Love,
Released from itself, blows words of love all over,
Now your hands are crossed down there.

We wanted your whole body behind glass,
And you left just half a footprint,
Half-smiling.

All night, driving,
I wanted to know:
At the turn of light that somewhere
Must still be cock's crow

You smiled slantwise in the side mirror,
Six months dead: *here's Romance*:
You wanted to know.

You Never, you blazing
Negative, o you wavering light in water,
Water I stir up with a stick: wavering rot,

O my sister!
          even if I'd known,
All I could have said was that I know.

Final Notations

ADRIENNE RICH

it will not be simple, it will not be long
it will take little time, it will take all your thought
it will take all your heart, it will take all your breath
it will be short, it will not be simple

it will touch through your ribs, it will take all your heart
it will not be long, it will occupy your thought
as a city is occupied, as a bed is occupied
it will take all your flesh, it will not be simple

You are coming into us who cannot withstand you
you are coming into us who never wanted to withstand you
you are taking parts of us into places never planned
you are going far away with pieces of our lives

it will be short, it will take all your breath
it will not be simple, it will become your will

One Continuous Substance

ALBERT GOLDBARTH

A small boy and a slant of morning light
both exit the last dark trees of this forest, though
the boy is gone in an instant. Not

the light: it travels its famous 186,000 miles per second
to be this still gold bar
on the floor of the darkness. I suppose

that from the universe's point of view
we do the same: a small boy and an old man
being one continuous substance.

We were making love when the phone rang
saying my father was dead, and the sun
kept touching you, there, and there, where I'd been.

Iron

JANE COOPER

Every morning I wake
with blood on my pillow
and the taste of fresh blood
like iron against my tongue.

They say my gums are inflamed
and the bleeding will cease
at first frost—
Each morning the sun wakes me.

I think some nerve is exposed—
it is only August—
or a fine skin was peeled off
the night you were killed.

Conversations at breakfast
have the stripped truth of poems.
All day I wait
for a miraculous letter.

In fact my whole life
leans forward slightly, waiting.
Each day lurches downhill
to its red undoing.

Bereavement

KEVIN YOUNG

Behind his house, my father's dogs
sleep in kennels, beautiful,
he built just for them.

They do not bark.
Do they know he is dead?
They wag their tails

& head. They beg
& are fed.
Their grief is colossal

& forgetful.
Each day they wake
seeking his voice,

their names.
By dusk they seem
to unremember everything—

to them even hunger
is a game. For that, I envy.
For that, I cannot bear to watch them

pacing their cage. I try to remember
they love best confined space
to feel safe. Each day

a saint comes by to feed the pair
& I draw closer
the shades.

I've begun to think of them
as my father's other sons,
as kin. Brothers-in-paw.

My eyes each day thaw.
One day the water cuts off.
Then back on.

They are outside dogs—
which is to say, healthy
& victorious, purposeful

& one giant muscle
like the heart. Dad taught
them not to bark, to point

out their prey. To stay.
Were they there that day?
They call me

like witnesses & will not say.
I ask for their care
& their carelessness—

wish of them forgiveness.
I must give them away.
I must find for them homes,

sleep restless in his.
All night I expect they pace
as I do, each dog like an eye

roaming with the dead
beneath an unlocked lid.

This Hour and What Is Dead

LI-YOUNG LEE

Tonight my brother, in heavy boots, is walking
through bare rooms over my head,
opening and closing doors.
What could he be looking for in an empty house?
What could he possibly need there in heaven?
Does he remember his earth, his birthplace set to torches?
His love for me feels like spilled water
running back to its vessel.

At this hour, what is dead is restless
and what is living is burning.

Someone tell him he should sleep now.

My father keeps a light on by our bed
and readies for our journey.
He mends ten holes in the knees
of five pairs of boy's pants.
His love for me is like his sewing:
various colors and too much thread,
the stitching uneven. But the needle pierces
clean through with each stroke of his hand.

At this hour, what is dead is worried
and what is living is fugitive.

Someone tell him he should sleep now.

God, that old furnace, keeps talking
with his mouth of teeth,
a beard stained at feasts, and his breath
of gasoline, airplane, human ash.
His love for me feels like fire,
feels like doves, feels like river-water.

At this hour, what is dead is helpless, kind
and helpless. While the Lord lives.

Someone tell the Lord to leave me alone.
I've had enough of his love
that feels like burning and flight and running away.

[Carrion Comfort]

GERARD MANLEY HOPKINS

Not, I'll not, carrion comfort, Despair, not feast on thee;
Not untwist—slack they may be—these last strands of man
In me ór, most weary, cry *I can no more*. I can;
Can something, hope, wish day come, not choose not to be.
But ah, but O thou terrible, why wouldst thou rude on me
Thy wring-world right foot rock? lay a lionlimb against me? scan
With darksome devouring eyes my bruisèd bones? and fan,
O in turns of tempest, me heaped there; me frantic to avoid
       thee and flee?

   Why? That my chaff might fly; my grain lie, sheer and clear.
Nay in all that toil, that coil, since (seems) I kissed the rod,
Hand rather, my heart lo! lapped strength, stole joy, would laugh,
       chéer.
Cheer whom though? The hero whose heaven-handling flung me,
       fóot tród
Me? or me that fought him? O which one? is it each one? That night,
       that year
Of now done darkness I wretch lay wrestling with (my God!) my God.

from Choir Practice

FORREST HAMER

*Thomas A. Dorsey wrote the song "Take My Hand, Precious Lord"
in 1932, just after his wife and newborn son had died.*

He must have hated the Lord.

Must have hated the Lord who loved him
so much he would take away his only child
and wife to have him, this Lord
who loved him too much to let him love.

Must have hated the Lord who forsaked
him, disbelief stunning the will, will stunned
by this betrayal.

Hatred must have rushed full against his ears like noise,
loud sound leaving him deaf.
So much he could not speak.

He must have dropped, felled
from some arrogance he did not imagine
could disturb Him.

Must have drowned himself in memory of her—
ache she had for the new one, one within,
giving her first dreams of calm
water, given, listening. Children:

He must have hated the Lord so much he could not stand
but love Him.

To Bhain Campbell

JOHN BERRYMAN

1911–1940

I told a lie once in a verse. I said
I said I said I said "The heart will mend,
Body will break and mend, the foam replace
For even the unconsolable his taken friend."
This is a lie. I had not been here then.

Epilogue

JOHN BERRYMAN

He died in December. He must descend
Somewhere, vague and cold, the spirit and seal,
The gift descend, and all that insight fail
Somewhere. Imagination one's one friend
Cannot see there. Both of us at the end.
Nouns, verbs do not exist for what I feel.

Sea Canes

DEREK WALCOTT

Half my friends are dead.
I will make you new ones, said earth.
No, give me them back, as they were, instead,
with faults and all, I cried.

Tonight I can snatch their talk
from the faint surf's drone
through the canes, but I cannot walk

on the moonlit leaves of ocean
down that white road alone,
or float with the dreaming motion

of owls leaving earth's load.
O earth, the number of friends you keep
exceeds those left to be loved.

The sea canes by the cliff flash green and silver,
they were the seraph lances of my faith,
but out of what is lost grows something stronger

that has the rational radiance of stone,
enduring moonlight, further than despair,
strong as the wind, that through dividing canes

brings those we love before us, as they were,
with faults and all, not nobler, just there.

Autumn Passage

ELIZABETH ALEXANDER

On suffering, which is real.
On the mouth that never closes,
the air that dries the mouth.

On the miraculous dying body,
its greens and purples.
On the beauty of hair itself.

On the dazzling toddler:
"Like eggplant," he says,
when you say "Vegetable,"

"Chrysanthemum" to "Flower."
On his grandmother's suffering, larger
than vanished skyscrapers,

September zucchini,
other things too big. For her glory
that goes along with it,

glory of grown children's vigil,
communal fealty, glory
of the body that operates

even as it falls apart, the body
that can no longer even make fever
but nonetheless burns

florid and bright and magnificent
as it dims, as it shrinks,
as it turns to something else.

Let Evening Come

JANE KENYON

Let the light of late afternoon
shine through chinks in the barn, moving
up the bales as the sun moves down.

Let the cricket take up chafing
as a woman takes up her needles
and her yarn. Let evening come.

Let dew collect on the hoe abandoned
in long grass. Let the stars appear
and the moon disclose her silver horn.

Let the fox go back to its sandy den.
Let the wind die down. Let the shed
go black inside. Let evening come.

To the bottle in the ditch, to the scoop
in the oats, to air in the lung
let evening come.

Let it come, as it will, and don't
be afraid. God does not leave us
comfortless, so let evening come.

II.
Regret

I believe, but what is belief?
—ANNE STEVENSON

Nothing Gold Can Stay

ROBERT FROST

Nature's first green is gold,
Her hardest hue to hold.
Her early leaf's a flower;
But only so an hour.
Then leaf subsides to leaf,
So Eden sank to grief,
So dawn goes down to day,
Nothing gold can stay.

The Spots

JOEL BROUWER

Appeared to her in Massachusetts. Purple and green.
And immediately

vertigo rushed up like an angry dog
to a fence. She went white, fell down the well

of herself and wept.
Late at night, in the motels, when she'd fallen

asleep, I cried too. I whispered curses to the awkward stacks
of white towels. Hating anything out of balance. Hating

her, her new failure. In the mornings
my checkbook voice returned, low and soft. For an angry dog

whose yard you wish to cross.
We both hated my balance, hated her imbalance, needed each.

Sudafed acupuncture ear candle.
Yoga chewing gum Zoloft Chinese tea.

She was afraid of going blind. She constantly described
colors and shapes, as if I had gone blind.

They turned orange. They floated. They darted.
We went arm in arm without passion, like elderly French.

Internist neurologist ophthalmologist.
Otolaryngologist neurologist psychiatrist.

She would not allow the warm towel over her face in the MRI.
The nurses seethed. She set her jaw and vanished

into the gleaming white tube. The machine banged like hammers
on a sunken ship's hull. She listened to Beethoven through
        headphones.

The magnetism passed through her mind in waves,
like wind through chestnut trees, touching

everything and changing nothing. Her courage! If courage
is what stones have. My God, how I loved her. Badly.

The spots were like metaphors. They told us something
by showing us something else. And so I believed they were metaphors.

They were not.

Like

FRANK BIDART

Woe is blunted not erased
by *like*. Your hands were too full, then

empty. At the grave's

lip, secretly you imagine then
refuse to imagine

a spectre

so like what you watched die, the unique
soul you loved endures a second death.

The dead hate *like*, bitter

when the living with too-small
grief replace them. You dread

loving again, exhausted by the hungers

ineradicable in his presence. *You resist
strangers until a stranger makes the old hungers*

brutally wake. We live by symbolic

substitution. At the grave's lip, what is
but is not is what

returns you to what is not.

Dreaming of the Dead

ANNE STEVENSON

(i.m. Anne Pennington)

I believe, but what is belief?

I receive the forbidden dead.
They appear in the mirrors of asleep
To accuse or be comforted.

All the selves of myself they keep,
From a bodiless time arrive,
Retaining in face and shape

Shifting lineaments of alive.
So whatever it is you are,
Dear Anne, bent smilingly grave

Over wine glasses filled by your fire,
Is the whole of your life you gave
To our fictions of what you were.

Not a shadow of you can save
These logs that crackle with light,
Or this smoky image I have—

Your face at the foot of a flight
Of wrought-iron circular stairs.
I am climbing alone in the night

Among stabbing, unmerciful flares.
Oh, I am what I see and know,
But no other solid thing's there

Except for the terrible glow
Of your face and its quiet belief,
Light wood ash falling like snow

On my weaker grief.

Grief

STEPHEN DOBYNS

Trying to remember you
is like carrying water
in my hands a long distance
across sand. Somewhere
people are waiting.
They have drunk nothing for days.

Your name was the food I lived on;
now my mouth is full of dirt and ash.
To say your name was to be surrounded
by feathers and silk; now, reaching out,
I touch glass and barbed wire.
Your name was the thread connecting my life;
now I am fragments on a tailor's floor.

I was dancing when I
learned of your death; may
my feet be severed from my body.

Elegy for Jane
(My student, thrown by a horse)

THEODORE ROETHKE

I remember the neckcurls, limp and damp as tendrils;
And her quick look, a sidelong pickerel smile;
And how, once startled into talk, the light syllables leaped for her,
And she balanced in the delight of her thought,

A wren, happy, tail into the wind,
Her song trembling the twigs and small branches.
The shade sang with her;
The leaves, their whispers turned to kissing,
And the mould sang in the bleached valleys under the rose.

Oh, when she was sad, she cast herself down into such a pure depth,
Even a father could not find her:
Scraping her cheek against straw,
Stirring the clearest water.

My sparrow, you are not here,
Waiting like a fern, making a spiney shadow.
The sides of wet stones cannot console me,
Nor the moss, wound with the last light.

If only I could nudge you from this sleep,
My maimed darling, my skittery pigeon.
Over this damp grave I speak the words of my love:
I, with no rights in this matter,
Neither father nor lover.

On the Death of Friends in Childhood

DONALD JUSTICE

We shall not ever meet them bearded in heaven,
Nor sunning themselves among the bald of hell;
If anywhere, in the deserted schoolyard at twilight,
Forming a ring, perhaps, or joining hands
In games whose very names we have forgotten.
Come, memory, let us seek them there in the shadows.

The Shout

SIMON ARMITAGE

We went out
into the school yard together, me and the boy
whose name and face

I don't remember. We were testing the range
of the human voice:
he had to shout for all he was worth,

I had to raise an arm
from across the divide to signal back
that the sound had carried.

He called from over the park—I lifted an arm.
Out of bounds,
he yelled from the end of the road,

from the foot of the hill,
from beyond the look-out post of Fretwell's Farm—
I lifted an arm.

He left town, went on to be twenty years dead
with a gunshot hole
in the roof of his mouth, in Western Australia.

Boy with the name and face I don't remember,
you can stop shouting now, I can still hear you.

We Assume: On the Death of Our Son, Reuben Masai Harper

MICHAEL S. HARPER

We assume
that in twenty-eight hours,
lived in a collapsible isolette,
you learned to accept pure oxygen
as the natural sky;
the scant shallow breaths
that filled those hours
cannot, did not make you fly—
but dreams were there
like crooked palmprints on
the twin-thick windows of the nursery—
in the glands of your mother.

We assume
the sterile hands
drank chemicals in and out
from lungs opaque with mucus,
pumped your stomach,
eeked the bicarbonate in
crooked, green-winged veins,
out in a plastic mask;

A woman who'd lost her first son
consoled us with an angel gone ahead
to pray for our family—
gone into that sky
seeking oxygen,
gone into autopsy,

a fine brown powdered sugar,
a disposable cremation:

We assume
you did not know we loved you.

Written on the Due Date of a Son Never Born

DAVID WOJAHN

Echinacea, bee balm, aster. Trumpet vine
I watch your mother bend to prune, water

sluicing silver from the hose—
                                     another morning
you will never see. Summer solstice: dragonflies flare

the unpetaled rose. 6 a.m.
                          & already
she's breaking down, hose flung to the sidewalk

where it snakes & pulses in a steady
keening glitter, both hands to her face. That much

I can give you of these hours.
                               That much only.
Fist & blossom forged by salt, trellising

your wounded helixes against our days,
tell us how to live
                     for we are shades, facing

caged the chastening sun. Our eyes
are scorched & lidless. We cannot bear your light.

Stillbirth

LAURE-ANNE BOSSELAAR

On a platform, I heard someone call out your name:
No, Laetitia, no.
It wasn't my train—the doors were closing,
but I rushed in, searching for your face.

But no Laetitia. No.
No one in that car could have been you,
but I rushed in, searching for your face:
no longer an infant. A woman now, blond, thirty-two.

No one in that car could have been you.
Laetitia-Marie was the name I had chosen.
No longer an infant. A woman now, blond, thirty-two:
I sometimes go months without remembering you.

Laetitia-Marie was the name I had chosen:
I was told not to look. Not to get attached—
I sometimes go months without remembering you.
Some griefs bless us that way, not asking much space.

I was told not to look. Not to get attached.
It wasn't my train—the doors were closing.
Some griefs bless us that way, not asking much space.
On a platform, I heard someone calling your name.

Mid-Term Break

SEAMUS HEANEY

I sat all morning in the college sick bay
Counting bells knelling classes to a close.
At two o'clock our neighbours drove me home.

In the porch I met my father crying—
He had always taken funerals in his stride—
And Big Jim Evans saying it was a hard blow.

The baby cooed and laughed and rocked the pram
When I came in, and I was embarrassed
By old men standing up to shake my hand

And tell me they were "sorry for my trouble."
Whispers informed strangers I was the eldest,
Away at school, as my mother held my hand

In hers and coughed out angry tearless sighs.
At ten o'clock the ambulance arrived
With the corpse, stanched and bandaged by the nurses.

Next morning I went up into the room. Snowdrops
And candles soothed the bedside; I saw him
For the first time in six weeks. Paler now,

Wearing a poppy bruise on his left temple,
He lay in the four foot box as in his cot.
No gaudy scars, the bumper knocked him clear.

A four foot box, a foot for every year.

A Litany

GREGORY ORR

I remember him falling beside me,
the dark stain already seeping across his parka hood.
I remember screaming and running the half mile to our house.
I remember hiding in my room.
I remember that it was hard to breathe
and that I kept the door shut in terror that someone would enter.
I remember pressing my knuckles into my eyes.
I remember looking out the window once
at where an ambulance had backed up
over the lawn to the front door.
I remember someone hung from a tree near the barn
the deer we'd killed just before I shot my brother.
I remember toward evening someone came with soup.
I slurped it down, unable to look up.
In the bowl, among the vegetable chunks,
pale shapes of the alphabet bobbed at random
or lay in the shallow spoon.

How Some of It Happened

MARIE HOWE

My brother was afraid, even as a boy, of going blind—so deeply
that he would turn the dinner knives away from, *looking at him,*

he said, as they lay on the kitchen table.
He would throw a sweatshirt over those knobs that lock the car door

from the inside, and once, he dismantled a chandelier in the middle
of the night when everyone was sleeping.

We found the pile of sharp and shining crystals in the upstairs hall.
So you understand, it was terrible

when they clamped his one eye open and put the needle in through
       his cheek
and up and into his eye from underneath

and left it there for a full minute before they drew it slowly out
once a week for many weeks. He learned to, *lean into it,*

to *settle down* he said, and still the eye went dead, ulcerated,
breaking up green in his head, as the other eye, still blue

and wide open, looked and looked at the clock.

My brother promised me he wouldn't die after our father died.
He shook my hand on a train going home one Christmas and gave me
       five years,

as clearly as he promised he'd be home for breakfast when I watched
    him
walk into that New York City autumn night. *By nine, I promise,*

and he was—he did come back. And five years later he promised five
    years more.
So much for the brave pride of premonition,

the worry that won't let it happen.
You know, he said, I always knew I would die young. And then I got
    sober

and I thought, OK, I'm not. I'm going to see thirty and live to be an old
    man.
And now it turns out that I am going to die. Isn't that funny?

—One day it happens: what you have feared all your life,
the unendurably specific, the exact thing. No matter what you say or do.

This is what my brother said: Here, sit closer to the bed
so I can see you.

Freedom, New Hampshire

GALWAY KINNELL

For my brother, 1925–1957

1

We came to visit the cow
Dying of fever,
Towle said it was already
Shoveled under, in a secret
Burial-place in the woods.
We prowled through the woods
Weeks, we never

Found where. Other
Children other summers
Must have found the place
And asked, Why is it
Green here? The rich
Guess a grave, maybe,
The poor think a pit

For dung, like the one
We shoveled in in the fall
That came up green
The next year, and that,
For all that shows, may as well
Have been the grave
Of a cow or something.

2

We found a cowskull once; we thought it was
From one of the asses in the Bible, for the sun
Shone into the holes through which it had seen
Earth as an endless belt carrying gravel, had heard
Its truculence cursed, had learned how sweat
Stinks, and had brayed—shone into the holes
With solemn and majestic light, as if some
Skull somewhere could be Baalbek or the Parthenon.

That night passing Towle's Barn
We saw lights. Towle had lassoed a calf
By its hind legs, and he tugged against the grip
Of the darkness. The cow stood by chewing millet.
Derry and I took hold, too, and hauled.
It was sopping with darkness when it came free.
It was a bullcalf. The cow mopped it awhile,
And we walked around it with a lantern,

And it was sunburned, somehow, and beautiful.
It took a dug as the first business
And sneezed and drank at the milk of light.
When we got it balanced on its legs, it went wobbling
Toward the night. Walking home in darkness
We saw the July moon looking on Freedom, New Hampshire,
We smelled the fall in the air, it was the summer,
We thought, Oh this is but the summer!

Once I saw the moon
Drift into the sky like a bright
Pregnancy pared
From a goddess doomed
To keep slender to be beautiful—

Cut loose, and drifting up there
To happen by itself—
And waning, in lost labor;

As we lost our labor
Too—afternoons
When we sat on the gate
By the pasture, under the Ledge,
Buzzing and skirling on toilet-
papered combs tunes
To the rumble-seated cars
Taking the Ossipee Road

On Sundays; for
Though dusk would come upon us
Where we sat, and though we had
Skirled out our hearts in the music,
Yet the dandruffed
Harps we skirled it on
Had done not much better than
Flies, which buzzed, when quick

We trapped them in our hands,
Which went silent when we
Crushed them, which we bore
Downhill to the meadowlark's
Nest full of throats
Which Derry charmed and combed
With an Arabian air, while I
Chucked crushed flies into

Innards I could not see,
For the night had fallen
And the crickets shrilled on all sides

In waves, as if the grassleaves
Shrieked by hillsides
As they grew, and the stars
Made small flashes in the sky,
Like mica flashing in rocks

On the chokecherried Ledge
Where bees I stepped on once
Hit us from behind like a shotgun,
And where we could see
Windowpanes in Freedom flash
And Loon Lake and Winnipesaukee
Flash in the sun
And the blue world flashing.

4

The fingerprints of our eyeballs would zigzag
On the sky; the clouds that came drifting up
Our fingernails would drift into the thin air;
In bed at night there was music if you listened,
Of an old surf breaking far away in the blood.

Children who come by chance on grass green for a man
Can guess cow, dung, man, anything they want,
To them it is the same. To us who knew him as he was
After the beginning and before the end, it is green
For a name called out of the confusions of the earth—

Winnipesaukee coined like a moon, a bullcalf
Dragged from the darkness where it breaks up again,
Larks which long since have crashed for good in the grass
To which we fed the flies, buzzing ourselves like flies,
While the crickets shrilled beyond us, in July . . .

The mind may sort it out and give it names—
When a man dies he dies trying to say without slurring
The abruptly decaying sounds. It is true
That only flesh dies, and spirit flowers without stop
For men, cows, dung, for all dead things; and it is good, yes—

But an incarnation is in particular flesh
And the dust that is swirled into a shape
And crumbles and is swirled again had but one shape
That was this man. When he is dead the grass
Heals what he suffered, but he remains dead,
And the few who loved him know this until they die.

Ice

MARY OLIVER

My father spent his last winter
Making ice-grips for shoes

Out of strips of inner tube and scrap metal.
(A device which slips over the instep

And holds under the shoe
A section of roughened metal, it allows you to walk

Without fear of falling
Anywhere on ice or snow.) My father

Should not have been doing
All that close work

In the drafty workshop, but as though
He sensed travel at the edge of his mind,

He would not be stopped. My mother
Wore them, and my aunt, and my cousins.

He wrapped and mailed
A dozen pairs to me, in the easy snows

Of Massachusetts, and a dozen
To my sister, in California.

Later we learned how he'd given them away
To the neighbors, an old man

Appearing with cold blue cheeks at every door.
No one refused him,

For plainly the giving was an asking,
A petition to be welcomed and useful—

Or maybe, who knows, the seed of a desire
Not to be sent alone out over the black ice.

Now the house seems neater: books,
Half-read, set back on the shelves;

Unfinished projects put away.
This spring

Mother writes to me: I am cleaning the workshop
And I have found

So many pairs of the ice-grips,
Cartons and suitcases stuffed full,

More than we can ever use.
What shall I do? And I see myself

Alone in that house with nothing
But darkly gleaming cliffs of ice, the sense

Of distant explosions,
Blindness as I look for my coat—

And I write back: Mother, please
Save everything.

The Last Hellos

LES MURRAY

Don't die, Dad—
but they die.

This last year he was wandery:
took off a new chainsaw blade
and cobbled a spare from bits.
Perhaps if I lay down
my head'll come better again.
His left shoulder kept rising
higher in his cardigan.

He could see death in a face.
Family used to call him in
to look at sick ones and say.
At his own time, he was told.

The knob found in his head
was duck-egg size. Never hurt.
Two to six months, Cecil.

I'll be right, he boomed
to his poor sister on the phone
I'll do that when I finish dyin.

Don't die, Cecil.
But they do.

Going for last drives
in the bush, odd massive

board-slotted stumps bony white
in whipstick second growth.
I could chop all day.

I could always cash
a cheque, in Sydney or anywhere.
Any of the shops.

Eating; still at the head
of the table, he now missed
food on his knife's side.

Sorry, Dad, but like
have you forgiven your enemies?
Your father and all of them?
All his lifetime of hurt.

I must have (grin). *I don't*
think about that now.

People can't say goodbye
any more. They say last hellos.

Going fast, over Christmas,
he'd still stumble out
of his room, where his photos
hang over the other furniture,
and play host to his mourners.

The courage of his bluster,
firm big voice of his confusion.

Two last days in the hospital:
his long forearms were still
red mahogany. His hands
gripped steel frame. *I'm dyin.*

On the second day:
You're bustin to talk
but I'm too busy dyin.

———

Grief ended when he died,
the widower like soldiers who
won't live life their mates missed.

Good boy Cecil! No more Bluey dog.
No more cowtime. No more stories.
We're still using your imagination,
it was stronger than all ours.

Your grave's got littler
somehow, in the three months.
More pointy as the clay's shrivelled,
like a stuck zip in a coat.

Your cricket boots are in
the State museum! Odd letters
still come. Two more's died since you:
Annie, and Stewart. Old Stewart.

On your day there was a good crowd,
family, and people from away.

But of course a lot had gone
to their own funerals first.

Snobs mind us off religion
nowadays, if they can.
Fuck thém. I wish you God.

"oh antic God"

LUCILLE CLIFTON

oh antic God
return to me
my mother in her thirties
leaned across the front porch
the huge pillow of her breasts
pressing against the rail
summoning me in for bed.

I am almost the dead woman's age times two.

I can barely recall her song
the scent of her hands
though her wild hair scratches my dreams
at night.   return to me, oh Lord of then
and now, my mother's calling,
her young voice humming my name.

Speaking to My Dead Mother

RUTH STONE

At two A.M. in Binghamton, it's quiet.
I did not comfort you with one last kiss.
Your death was my death. Instinct ran riot.
I ran. Didn't hold your hand at the abyss.
My life had gone like grass fire; like the trees
in drought, caught in the burning wind. And June
returns, another cycled year. Sweet-peas,
dahlias, phlox; the orchard I can't prune;
your small garden gloves, remnants of crystal
stemware. It wears away. I cannot bar
the passage. Jewelweed shoots its pistol
pouch of seeds and the storm, like a guitar,
thrums over the mountain. All that brooded,
ignorant in your safe arms, concluded.

The Reassurance

THOM GUNN

About ten days or so
After we saw you dead
You came back in a dream.
I'm all right now you said.

And it *was* you, although
You were fleshed out again:
You hugged us all round then,
And gave your welcoming beam.

How like you to be kind,
Seeking to reassure.
And, yes, how like my mind
To make itself secure.

My Sister, Who Died Young, Takes Up the Task

JON PINEDA

A basket of apples brown in our kitchen,
their warm scent is the scent of ripening,

and my sister, entering the room quietly,
takes a seat at the table, takes up the task

of peeling slowly away the blemished skins,
even half-rotten ones are salvaged carefully.

She makes sure to carve out the mealy flesh.
For this, I am grateful. I explain, *this elegy*

would love to save everything. She smiles at me,
and before long, the empty bowl she uses fills,

domed with thin slices she brushes into
the mouth of a steaming pot on the stove.

What can I do? I ask finally. *Nothing,*
she says, *let me finish this one thing alone.*

Elegy for My Father

MARK STRAND

Robert Strand 1908–1968

1

THE EMPTY BODY

The hands were yours, the arms were yours,
But you were not there.
The eyes were yours, but they were closed and would not open.
The distant sun was there.
The moon poised on the hill's white shoulder was there.
The wind on Bedford Basin was there.
The pale green light of winter was there.
Your mouth was there,
But you were not there.
When somebody spoke, there was no answer.
Clouds came down
And buried the buildings along the water,
And the water was silent.
The gulls stared.
The years, the hours, that would not find you
Turned in the wrists of others.
There was no pain. It had gone.
There were no secrets. There was nothing to say.
The shade scattered its ashes.
The body was yours, but you were not there.
The air shivered against its skin.
The dark leaned into its eyes.
But you were not there.

2
ANSWERS

Why did you travel?
Because the house was cold.
Why did you travel?
Because it is what I have always done between sunset and sunrise.
What did you wear?
I wore a blue suit, a white shirt, yellow tie, and yellow socks.
What did you wear?
I wore nothing. A scarf of pain kept me warm.
Who did you sleep with?
I slept with a different woman each night.
Who did you sleep with?
I slept alone. I have always slept alone.
Why did you lie to me?
I always thought I told the truth.
Why did you lie to me?
Because the truth lies like nothing else and I love the truth.
Why are you going?
Because nothing means much to me anymore.
Why are you going?
I don't know. I have never known.
How long shall I wait for you?
Do not wait for me. I am tired and I want to lie down.
Are you tired and do you want to lie down?
Yes, I am tired and I want to lie down.

3
YOUR DYING

Nothing could stop you.
Not the best day. Not the quiet. Not the ocean rocking.
You went on with your dying.

Not the trees
Under which you walked, not the trees that shaded you.
Not the doctor
Who warned you, the white-haired young doctor who saved
      you once.
You went on with your dying.
Nothing could stop you. Not your son. Not your daughter
Who fed you and made you into a child again.
Not your son who thought you would live forever.
Not the wind that shook your lapels.
Not the stillness that offered itself to your motion.
Not your shoes that grew heavier.
Not your eyes that refused to look ahead.
Nothing could stop you.
You sat in your room and stared at the city
And went on with your dying.
You went to work and let the cold enter your clothes.
You let blood seep into your socks.
Your face turned white.
Your voice cracked in two.
You leaned on your cane.
But nothing could stop you.
Not your friends who gave you advice.
Not your son. Not your daughter who watched you grow small.
Not fatigue that lived in your sighs.
Not your lungs that would fill with water.
Not your sleeves that carried the pain of your arms.
Nothing could stop you.
You went on with your dying.
When you played with children you went on with your dying.
When you sat down to eat,
When you woke up at night, wet with tears, your body sobbing,
You went on with your dying.
Nothing could stop you.

Not the past.
Not the future with its good weather.
Not the view from your window, the view of the graveyard.
Not the city. Not the terrible city with its wooden buildings.
Not defeat. Not success.
You did nothing but go on with your dying.
You put your watch to your ear.
You felt yourself slipping.
You lay on the bed.
You folded your arms over your chest and you dreamed of the world
        without you,
Of the space under the trees,
Of the space in your room,
Of the spaces that would now be empty of you,
And you went on with your dying.
Nothing could stop you.
Not your breathing. Not your life.
Not the life you wanted.
Not the life you had.
Nothing could stop you.

4
YOUR SHADOW

You have your shadow.
The places where you were have given it back.
The hallways and bare lawns of the orphanage have given it back.
The Newsboys' Home has given it back.
The streets of New York have given it back and so have the streets of
        Montreal.
The rooms in Belém where lizards would snap at mosquitoes have
        given it back.
The dark streets of Manaus and the damp streets of Rio have given it
        back.

Mexico City where you wanted to leave it has given it back.

And Halifax where the harbor would wash its hands of you has given it back.

You have your shadow.

When you traveled the white wake of your going sent your shadow below, but when you arrived it was there to greet you. You had your shadow.

The doorways you entered lifted your shadow from you and when you went out, gave it back. You had your shadow.

Even when you forgot your shadow, you found it again; it had been with you.

Once in the country the shade of a tree covered your shadow and you were not known.

Once in the country you thought your shadow had been cast by somebody else. Your shadow said nothing.

Your clothes carried your shadow inside; when you took them off, it spread like the dark of your past.

And your words that float like leaves in an air that is lost, in a place no one knows, gave you back your shadow.

Your friends gave you back your shadow.

Your enemies gave you back your shadow. They said it was heavy and would cover your grave.

When you died your shadow slept at the mouth of the furnace and ate ashes for bread.

It rejoiced among ruins.

It watched while others slept.

It shone like crystal among the tombs.

It composed itself like air.

It wanted to be like snow on water.

It wanted to be nothing, but that was not possible.

It came to my house.

It sat on my shoulders.

Your shadow is yours. I told it so. I said it was yours.

I have carried it with me too long. I give it back.

5

MOURNING

They mourn for you.
When you rise at midnight,
And the dew glitters on the stone of your cheeks,
They mourn for you.
They lead you back into the empty house.
They carry the chairs and tables inside.
They sit you down and teach you to breathe.
And your breath burns,
It burns the pine box and the ashes fall like sunlight.
They give you a book and tell you to read.
They listen and their eyes fill with tears.
The women stroke your fingers.
They comb the yellow back into your hair.
They shave the frost from your beard.
They knead your thighs.
They dress you in fine clothes.
They rub your hands to keep them warm.
They feed you. They offer you money.
They get on their knees and beg you not to die.
When you rise at midnight they mourn for you.
They close their eyes and whisper your name over and over.
But they cannot drag the buried light from your veins.
Old man, rise and keep rising, it does no good.
They mourn for you the way they can.

6

THE NEW YEAR

It is winter and the new year.
Nobody knows you.
Away from the stars, from the rain of light,

You lie under the weather of stones.
There is no thread to lead you back.
Your friends doze in the dark
Of pleasure and cannot remember.
Nobody knows you. You are the neighbor of nothing.
You do not see the rain falling and the man walking away,
The soiled wind blowing its ashes across the city.
You do not see the sun dragging the moon like an echo.
You do not see the bruised heart go up in flames,
The skulls of the innocent turn into smoke.
You do not see the scars of plenty, the eyes without light.
It is over. It is winter and the new year.
The meek are hauling their skins into heaven.
The hopeless are suffering the cold with those who have nothing to
        hide.
It is over and nobody knows you.
There is starlight drifting on the black water.
There are stones in the sea no one has seen.
There is a shore and people are waiting.
And nothing comes back.
Because it is over.
Because there is silence instead of a name.
Because it is winter and the new year.

Men at My Father's Funeral

WILLIAM MATTHEWS

The ones his age who shook my hand
on their way out sent fear along
my arm like heroin. These weren't
men mute about their feelings,
or what's a body language for?

And I, the glib one, who'd stood
with my back to my father's body
and praised the heart that attacked him?
I'd made my stab at elegy,
the flesh made word: the very spit

in my mouth was sour with ruth
and eloquence. What could be worse?
Silence, the anthem of my father's
new country. And thus this babble,
like a dial tone, from our bodies.

On the Death of a Colleague

STEPHEN DUNN

She taught theater, so we gathered
in the theater.
We praised her voice, her knowledge,
how good she was
with *Godot* and just four months later
with *Gigi*.
She was fifty. The problem in the liver.
Each of us recalled
an incident in which she'd been kind
or witty.
I told about being unable to speak
from my diaphragm
and how she made me lie down, placed her hand
where the failure was
and showed me how to breathe.
But afterwards
I only could do it when I lay down
and that became a joke
between us, and I told it as my offering
to the audience.
I was on stage and I heard myself
wishing to be impressive.
Someone else spoke of her cats
and no one spoke
of her face or the last few parties.
The fact was
I had avoided her for months.

It was a student's turn to speak, a sophomore,
one of her actors.
She was a drunk, he said, often came to class
reeking.
Sometimes he couldn't look at her, the blotches,
the awful puffiness.
And yet she was a great teacher,
he loved her,
but thought someone should say
what everyone knew
because she didn't die by accident.

Everyone was crying. Everyone was crying and it
was almost over now.
The remaining speaker, an historian, said he'd cut
his speech short.
And the Chairman stood up as if by habit,
said something about loss
and thanked us for coming. None of us moved
except some students
to the student who'd spoken, and then others
moved to him, across dividers,
down aisles, to his side of the stage.

Marquee Moon

JEFF FALLIS

For Peter Smith 1976–1999

Those halcyon days. All I did was
Drink and watch Hitchcock movies.
Bivouacked in your living room, transient,
I still got confused when I woke at night.
The evenings were chilly,
The backyard sloped down to the creekbed,
All the furniture had done different shades of yellow.
You'd come home from your girlfriend's every
Four or five days and we'd sit and talk
In the sunlight like two old men in the lobby
Of a hotel. We spun Stones and Yardbirds,
Swapped gossip about old bluesmen,
Watched the ice in our glasses melt.

Sometimes when you were gone,
I'd just stand in your room, amazed.
No bed, only a pillow on the floor,
All those albums lined up against the wall.
Disabled amplifiers sat with their guts
Spilling out of them, guitar necks longed
For bodies and strings, tools were scattered
Like ashes. Everything waited for you
To minister to its disconnectedness, everything
Felt alive and dead. And in the closet,
Your shirts and pants rested
On the same metal hangers,

The finest wardrobe in town:
Blues, brown, blues.

———

A photograph I saw
　　　　　months later:
you in your corduroy jacket,
　　　　　hair blond
as an old coin, lifting
　　　　　two fingers
into something like a
　　　　　great beyond.

———

　　　Night I got the news, London was raw & ugly. The next night it
snowed but didn't stick, that night it was just cold & wet. I already had
plans so I kept them: rode the Tube to Brixton w/ the wind knocked
out of me, found the club by accident. What happened? I don't know
what happened. I drank a double whiskey for you. Backstage they were
playing Television, you'd have liked that. I got lost on the night bus.
Trafalgar Square lit up like an open-air cathedral, all those drunks
changing routes and yelling at each other. I got stuck on Oxford St. for
an hour, didn't roll home till after five. Is it oblivion or Valhalla, Pete?
In bed I cried till my chest hurt.

———

And you won't snap your fingers again.
Won't talk with your hands, won't
Stand on the South Bank feeling lonely,
Won't go to matinees, won't eat fish,
Won't change brake pads, won't have
Children, won't get the mail, won't shoot up,
Won't nod out, won't turn the wrong color

97

In the back of a van, won't wake up in morning's arms
With the day in front of you like two-lane blacktop.

Or will you?
Will I run across your eyes in someone else's face,

glimpse by accident your silhouette
                         gliding across Prince Avenue,
shuffling under the slashed
                         network of the half-dark sky?

———

So Peter I give you this
But I know it's not enough—

You deserve an offering
Greater than what I can extend,

Something like
An undiscovered city on the moon

A stack of LP's cut loose from gravity

A clean white bed by a dirty river.

The Facts of Grief

JIM DANIELS

He fired a crabapple into my spokes.
I jumped off my bike and we wrestled
in the driveway, rolled onto the lawn.
My oldest friend.
                His daughter died
last week, blind, a hole in her heart.
14 years of diapers and a carseat.
She was the size of a 3 year old.

When he started punching me,
I grabbed his wrists to protest
but we'd crossed the line.
It wasn't chalk, but a crack in cement.

Carl Mackey was so dumb he thought
we were each other, or at least
brothers.
          Dumb gets redefined,
paper clouds arranged in the sky
to explain the absence of sun.
14 years, he bent to her weak heart
and listened.
               That was my last fight.
His mother came out and broke
it up. I wiped blood on my shirt
and shook his hand.
                 We're talking
about that today.

                    Not her.
                                        Not
laughing about it. Our first end
of the world. I'm clutching
the black phone in my fist. *Where
did those crabapples come from?*
he wonders. *We didn't have a tree.*

How long were we mad at each other?
It was a cardboard tree, and the apples
were lollipops. We were stick people
pasted on, our hearts colored
outside the lines,
                                spilling. My blood
was melted popsicles. *The coffin
was so light.*

We knelt together, altar boys
in the dim church, winter mornings.
We believed in everything. What
do I say? I flip clichés like soiled
playing cards, the ends bent and frayed.

No tricks on this end.
                              Nobody
had a tree, I tell him. He could listen
all day to things like that,
breathing static on the other end.

David Lemieux

DENISE DUHAMEL

My first boyfriend is dead of AIDS. The one
who bought me a terrarium with a cactus
I watered until it became soft. The one

who took me to his junior high prom where I was shy
about dancing in public. The one who was mistaken
for a girl by a clerk when he wanted to try on a suit.

In seventh grade my first boyfriend and I looked a lot alike:
chubby arms, curly hair, our noses touching
when we tried our first kiss. My first boyfriend

was the only one who met my grandmother
before she died. Though, as a rule, she didn't like boys,
I think she liked my first boyfriend.

My first boyfriend and I sat in the backseat
of my mother's car, and on the ledge behind us
was a ceramic ballerina with a missing arm.

We were driving somewhere to have her repaired
or maybe to buy the right kind of glue.
My first boyfriend was rich and had horses

and airplanes he could fly by remote control.
My first boyfriend died on a mattress
thrown on the back of a pick-up

because the ambulance wouldn't come.
There was a garden in my first boyfriend's yard.
One day his mother said to us,

"Pick out some nice things for lunch."
My first boyfriend and I pulled at the carrot tops,
but all we came up with were little orange balls

that looked like kumquats without the bumps.
My first boyfriend and I heard ripping through the soil
that sounded close to our scalps, like a hair brush

through tangles. We were the ones who pushed
the tiny carrots back down, hoping they were able
to reconnect to the ground. We were the ones.

Dirge Without Music

EDNA ST. VINCENT MILLAY

I am not resigned to the shutting away of loving hearts in the
    hard ground.
So it is, and so it will be, for so it has been, time out of mind:
Into the darkness they go, the wise and the lovely. Crowned
With lilies and with laurel they go; but I am not resigned.

Lovers and thinkers, into the earth with you.
Be one with the dull, the indiscriminate dust.
A fragment of what you felt, of what you knew,
A formula, a phrase remains,—but the best is lost.

The answers quick and keen, the honest look, the laughter, the love,—
They are gone. They are gone to feed the roses. Elegant and curled
Is the blossom. Fragrant is the blossom. I know. But I do not approve.
More precious was the light in your eyes than all the roses in the
    world.

Down, down, down into the darkness of the grave
Gently they go, the beautiful, the tender, the kind;
Quietly they go, the intelligent, the witty, the brave.
I know. But I do not approve. And I am not resigned.

III.
Remembrance

What did I know, what did I know . . .
—ROBERT HAYDEN

After

ELIZABETH ALEXANDER

It wasn't as deep as I expected,
your grave, next to the grandmother who died
when I was three. I threw a flower in
and fizzled off the scene like carbonation.
My body of course remained but all else
was a cluster of tiny white bubbles
floating up, up, up, to an unseen top.

I wore your vicuna coat and an ill-
fitting cloche from Alexanders. I walked
among the rows, away from the men
covering the coffin, which was when I saw
"X," Malcolm, a few yards down, "Paul Robeson,"
then "Judy Garland" then—the car was waiting
and we had to go.

       The cocktail parties
must be something there! You'd discuss self-help
and the relative merits of Garvey-
ism with Malcolm. Robeson would read
in a corner. Judy, divine in black
clam-diggers, would throw back her head
and guffaw, smoke as many cigarettes
as she wanted.

       Before you died I dreamed
of cocktail parties in your Harlem
apartment where you'd bring all our dead kin

back to life, for me! I was old enough
to drink with you, to wear a cocktail dress.
Like the best movies, the dream was black
and white, except for my grandmother's
lipstick, which was red.

Poems for My Brother Kenneth

OWEN DODSON

I

I remember from your life: the senior laughter,
The senior laughter and the big stain
Death marked on the pillow where you died;
How the morning shadows came to hide
The bed
Where you lay—dead;
The horizontal smooth patterns of the maple coffin.

Later nights I dreamt you awoke
And took me by the hand
To the hall
Of the grave
And gave
Me duties to perform when I went out.
That was all.

Duties like remembering how to sit
Laughing at life by being part of it;
Like knitting long threads of laughter
To blanket the silence in the hall, Hereafter.

And I said: Is there some way to watch long tanks creep
Over the world with their iron sound and still sleep?
When the dark body of the ruined dark boy
Is ashes and bones, how can I talk with joy?

There was no reply:
You gave me a smile and returned to the grave.

II

Our country will not be in war again:
A mock-war played by children who dreamt of soldiers
And soldiers' houses in the earth,
Of banners and the great burning splash of rainbow shells
Drying the earth, the toy dead lying stiff
Staring their painted stare.
Immediate resurrection: the game was on again.
It was only a child war then!

III

Suddenly all the voices stopped,
Suddenly as you would blow a candle out
Or click the radio off,
The transmission ended;
The concert was over for the night.
I would hear again,
The announcer said,
In the morning . . . *the morning* . . .

IV

My chief citizen is dead
And my town at half-mast:
Even in speech,
Even in walking,
Even in seeing
The busy streets where he stood
And the room where he was host to his friends
And his enemies, where we erased the night to dawn
With conversation of what I had seen and he had seen
And done and written during the space of time we were apart.
We will not talk again with common breath.
His voice has gone to talk to death.
There is a new language to learn

And I am learning like a truant child.
I do not understand this code, this life to death.
I will not be convinced that we must
Only talk again as dust to dust.

V

If we had counted all the stars
And made each constellation clear,
I'd recognize more than this spear
Swinging from the solid side of Mars.

But when we went, not long ago
Exploring all that silver land,
I would not stay because the snow
Turned ice within my hand.

VI

Your memory is my star and my night.
The two shine contrapuntally, their music
I read in sounds, I read in listening:
All the pretensions we once thought so bright.

I knew you in the early days before
The words for freedom rang on stone,
And the high terrible sign of truth
Was all we wished and all we saw.

The vocabulary belongs to you now dead,
Whose language was deeper than life
And wider than the curve of sea
We scanned from this beach before this came instead.

My heart has no fountains to reach in air
To what was pure and singing in our life;

The music fountains stay below the earth,
And bomb-dust fountains burst truth everywhere.

VII

Sleep late with your dream.
The morning has a scar
To mark on the horizon
With the death of the morning star.

The color of blood will appear
And wash the morning sky,
Aluminum birds flying with fear
Will scream to your waking,
Will send you to die;

Sleep late with your dream.
Pretend that the morning is far,
Deep in the horizon country,
Unconcerned with the morning star.

VIII

Death, split-second guest, negative magician
When will you believe you are not final?
After you have touched a heart
And tricked it into silence,
Standing smooth and quiet by your side,
Memory robs you,
Picks your pockets clean,
Then rings her bells
And dances with the years.
Chemistry-master Death, mourn for yourself,
Mourn for your sad-Judas-wandering occupation,
Mourn for your swift silences, your stiffness,
Your company of worms,
Mourn for your own life, Death.

That body in the ground
With the chin set hard against the neck
Expanding the face,
The rigid shoulders,
The hands posed artificially,
Is awaiting nothing—
It has its final horizontal home.

Even though the sun comes only through the roots
Like vitamins, it does not matter.
There will be no resurrection: no eager Gabriel trumpet.
The resurrection is now, in Memory
Ringing all her jester bells;
Is now and for the ever of all my days.

IX

Here is holly for you, brother, here is mistletoe,
Here is the song we sing this Christmas with the cold sparrow.

We come with Christmas in our arms on the day of the original Child,
But woven in these blanket wreaths is sorrow, pared and wild.

It is almost a year now, nearing the twentieth day
Of the second month, when you died, so we will lay

Holly with berries, and hemlock washed and clean
For the earth to celebrate with us what you have been.

Artifact

CLAUDIA EMERSON

For three years you lived in your house
just as it was before she died: your wedding
portrait on the mantel, her clothes hanging
in the closet, her hair still in the brush.
You have told me you gave it all away
then, sold the house, keeping only the confirmation
cross she wore, her name in cursive chased
on the gold underside, your ring in the same

box, those photographs you still avoid,
and the quilt you spread on your borrowed bed—
small things. Months after we met, you told me she had
made it, after we had slept already beneath its loft
and thinning, raveled pattern, as though beneath
her shadow, moving with us, that dark, that soft.

Remember Me

HAL SIROWITZ

Every weekend your mother & I tour cemetery plots,
Father said, the way most people visit model homes.
We have different tastes. I like jutting hills
overlooking traffic, whereas she prefers a bed
of flowers. She desires a plot away from traffic noise.
I let her have her way in death to avoid a life of Hell.
But when you light memorial candles for us, arrange hers
in the center of a flowery tablecloth, but place mine
on the windowsill. Don't say any prayers for me,
just wet your finger, & pass it through the flame.
Remember me by the tricks I have taught you.

Death Is a Woman

JOY HARJO

I walk these night hours between the dead and the living, and see you
two-step with Death as if nothing ever ended.
We buried you in Okmulgee, on a day when leaves already buried
the earth in scarlet and crisp ochre.
Four years isn't long on this spiral of tangential stories.
I can already see my own death trying on my shoes
as clearly as I saw your young demise in the early fifties
as she tripped the street before you in high heels.
I smelled her sweet perfume like a carnival in my childhood
and knew even then you would never be satisfied
until you had her.
Tonight I see the tracks the sun makes at the fold of unreason,
a space where geese disappear like teeth behind the lips
of night.
       I am ready to run.
Instead I'll make up another story about who I think you really were
with the words left in the mouth of a cardinal
who startled us your last summer.
Six months later you flew from the sour trailer that dissolved
from metal to salt air, into her arms.
I see you dip and sway on the mythical dance floor
just the other side of this room of whirling atoms, my father
of Tiger people, who drank whiskey thrown back with bleached
      women
all of them blonde except for my Cherokee mother and the
      Pottowatamie
who once when you were dying gambled your money as you drove
      yourself

spitting blood to the hospital.
I have a photograph of you with my mother, from before
or after I was born.
Here you sit in Cain's Ballroom, reeking of Lucky Strikes
your hair slick and black as a beaver's, feeling better
than you could ever believe.
And my mother on the same side as your heart
looking past the camera, into her imagined future without you,
fiercely into the brutal eyes of the woman who seduced you
and won.
You are dancing with Death now, you were dancing with her then.
And there is nothing I could ever do about it.
Not then, or now.
I have nothing to prove your fierce life, except paper
that turns back to dust.
Except this song that plays over and over
that you keep dancing to.

Tiara

MARK DOTY

Peter died in a paper tiara
cut from a book of princess paper dolls;
he loved royalty, sashes

and jewels. *I don't know,*
he said, when he woke in the hospice,
I was watching the Bette Davis film festival

on Channel 57 and then—
At the wake, the tension broke
when someone guessed

the casket closed because
he was in there in a big wig
and heels, and someone said,

You know he's always late,
he probably isn't here yet—
he's still fixing his makeup.

And someone said he asked for it.
Asked for it—
when all he did was go down

into the salt tide
of wanting as much as he wanted,
giving himself over so drunk

or stoned it almost didn't matter who,
though they were beautiful,
stampeding into him in the simple,

ravishing music of their hurry.
I think heaven is perfect stasis
poised over the realms of desire,

where dreaming and waking men lie
on the grass while wet horses
roam among them, huge fragments

of the music we die into
in the body's paradise.
Sometimes we wake not knowing

how we came to lie here,
or who has crowned us with these temporary,
precious stones. And given

the world's perfectly turned shoulders,
the deep hollows blued by longing,
given the irreplaceable silk

of horses rippling in orchards,
fruit thundering and chiming down,
given the ordinary marvels of form

and gravity, what could he do,
what could any of us ever do
but ask for it?

A Memorial: Son Bret

WILLIAM STAFFORD

In the way you went you were important.
I do not know what you found.
In the pattern of my life you stand
where you stood always; in the center,
a hero, a puzzle, a man.

What you might have told me
I will never know—the lips went still,
the body cold. I am afraid,
in the circling stars, in the dark,
and even at noon in the light.

When I run what am I running from?
You turned once to tell me something,
but then you glimpsed a shadow on my face
and maybe thought, Why tell what hurts?
You carried it, my boy, so brave, so far.

Now we have all the days, and the sun
goes by the same; there is a faint,
wandering trail I find sometimes, off
through grass and sage. I stop
and listen: only summer again—remember?—

The bees, the wind.

The Morning Baking

CAROLYN FORCHÉ

Grandma, come back, I forgot
How much lard for these rolls

Think you can put yourself in the ground
Like plain potatoes and grow in Ohio?
I am damn sick of getting fat like you

Think you can lie through your Slovak?
Tell filthy stories about the blood sausage?
Pish-pish nights at the virgin in Detroit?

I blame your raising me up for my Slav tongue
You beat me up out back, taught me to dance

I'll tell you I don't remember any kind of bread
Your wavy loaves of flesh
Stink through my sleep
The stars on your silk robes

But I'm glad I'll look when I'm old
Like a gypsy dusha hauling milk

Hand Me Down Blues

CALVIN FORBES

for my brother George
1933–1971

Though I look like you
I never knew you very well.
You always confuse my slow shadow
And mock my fate.

I wear your defeats, limp or strut,
Even lie like you.
And I grow to fit your fears:
The carnivorous marriage,

And you swallowing a soft poison
Prescribed for healing
Only minor wounds.
I inherit new and old scars,

Dimples and warts; I am the residue
Of your black waste, its sin.
I am what remains
Beyond hunger or repair,

Your dead-ringer.
The worst lie is to say good-bye.
Where are you going that I won't follow?
My best is full of holes.

Grief

C. K. WILLIAMS

Dossie Williams, 1914–1995

1.

Gone now, after the days of desperate, unconscious gasping, the
    reflexive staying alive,

tumorous lungs, tumorous blood, ruined, tumorous liver demanding
    to live, to go on,

even the innocent bladder, its tenuous, dull golden coin in the slack
    translucent bag;

gone now, after the months of scanning, medication, nausea, hair loss
    and weight loss;

remission, partial remission, gratitude, hope, lost hope, anxiety, anger,
    confusion,

the hours and days of everyday life, something like life but only as
    dying is like life;

gone the quiet at the end of dying, the mouth caught agape on its last
    bite at a breath,

bare skull with its babylike growth of new hair thrown back to open
    the terrified larynx;

the flesh given way but still of the world, lost but still in the world with
    the living;

my hand on her face, on her brow, the sphere of her skull, her arm, so
    thin, so wasted;

gone, yet of us and with us, a person, not yet mere dream or imagina-
    tion, then, gone, wholly,

under the earth, cold earth, cold grasses, cold winter wind, freezing
    eternity, cold, forever.

2.

Is this grief? Tears took me, then ceased; the wish to die, too, may have
    fled through me,
but not more than with any moment's despair, the old, surging wish to
    be freed, finished.
I feel pain, pain for her fear, pain for her having to know she was going,
    though we must;
pain for the pain of my daughter and son, for my wife whose despair
    for her mother returned;
pain for all human beings who know they will go and still go as
    though they knew nothing,
even pain for myself, my incomprehension, my fear of stories never
    begun now never ending.
But still, is this grief: waking too early, tiring too quickly, distracted,
    impatient, abrupt,
but still waking, still thinking and working; is this what grief is, is this
    pain enough?
I go to the mirror: someone who might once have felt something
    merely regards me,
eyes telling nothing, mouth saying nothing, nothing reflected but the
    things of the world,
nothing told not of any week's, no, already ten days now, any ten days'
    normal doings.
Shouldn't the face evidence anguish, shouldn't its loving sadness and
    loss be revealed?
Ineffable, vague, elusive, uncertain, distracted: shouldn't grief have a
    form of its own,
and shouldn't mind know past its moment of vague, uncertain
    distraction the sureness of sorrow;
shouldn't soul flinch as we're taught proper souls are supposed to, in
    reverence and fear?
Shouldn't grief be pure and complete, reshaping the world in itself, in
    grief for itself?

3.

Eighty, dying, in bed, tubes in her chest, my mother puts on her
      morning makeup;
the broad, deft strokes of foundation, the blended-in rouge, powder,
      eye shadow, lipstick;
that concentration with which you must gaze at yourself, that raven-
      ous, unfaltering focus.
Grief for my mother, for whatever she thought her face had to be, to be
      made every morning;
grief for my mother-in-law in her last declining, destroying dementia,
      getting it wrong,
the thick ropes of rouge, garish green paint on her lips; mad, misplaced
      slash of mascara;
grief for all women's faces, applied, created, trying to manifest what
      the soul seeks to be;
grief for the faces of all human beings, our own faces telling us so
      much and no more,
offering pain to all who behold them, but which when they turn to
      themselves, petrify, pose.
Grief for the faces of adults who must gaze in their eyes deeply so as
      not to glimpse death,
and grief for the young who see only their own relentless and grievous
      longing for love.
Grief for my own eyes that try to seek truth, even of pain, of grief, but
      find only approximation.

4.

My face beneath your face, face of grief, countenance of loss, of fear, of
      irrevocable extinction;
matrix laid upon matrix, mystery on mystery, guise upon guise, sem-
      blance, effigy, likeness.
Oh; to put the face of grief on in the morning; the tinting, smoothing,
      shining and shaping;

and at the end of the day, to remove it, detach it, emerge from the
      sorrowful mask.
Stripped now of its raiment, the mouth, caught in its last labored
      breath, finds last resolution;
all the flesh now, stripped of its guises, moves towards its place in the
      peace of the earth.
Grief for the earth, accepting the grief of the flesh and the grief of our
      grieving forever;
grief for the flesh and the body and face, for the eyes that can see only
      into the world,
and the mind that can only think and feel what the world gives it to
      think and to feel;
grief for the mind gone, the flesh gone, the imperfect pain that must
      stay for its moment;
and grief for the moment, its partial beauties, its imperfect affections,
      all severed, all torn.

Myth

NATASHA TRETHEWEY

I was asleep while you were dying.
It's as if you slipped through some rift, a hollow
I make between my slumber and my waking,

the Erebus I keep you in, still trying
not to let go. You'll be dead again tomorrow,
but in dreams you live. So I try taking

you back into morning. Sleep-heavy, turning,
my eyes open, I find you do not follow.
Again and again, this constant forsaking.

———

Again and again, this constant forsaking:
my eyes open, I find you do not follow.
You back into morning, sleep-heavy, turning.

But in dreams you live. So I try taking,
not to let go. You'll be dead again tomorrow.
The Erebus I keep you in—still, trying—

I make between my slumber and my waking.
It's as if you slipped through some rift, a hollow.
I was asleep while you were dying.

The Bones of My Father

ETHERIDGE KNIGHT

1

There are no dry bones
here in this valley. The skull
of my father grins
at the Mississippi moon
from the bottom
of the Tallahatchie,
the bones of my father
are buried in the mud
of these creeks and brooks that twist
and flow their secrets to the sea.
but the wind sings to me
here the sun speaks to me
of the dry bones of my father.

2

There are no dry bones
in the northern valley, in the Harlem alleys
young/black/men with knees bent
nod on the stoops of the tenements
and dream
of the dry bones of my father.

And young white longhairs who flee
their homes, and bend their minds
and sing their songs of brotherhood
and no more wars are searching for
my father's bones.

3

There are no dry bones
here, my brothers. We hide from the sun.
No more do we take the long straight strides.
Our steps have been shaped by the cages
that kept us. We glide sideways
like crabs across the sand.
We perch on green lilies, we search
beneath white rocks. . . .
THERE ARE NO DRY BONES HERE

The skull of my father
grins at the Mississippi moon
from the bottom
of the Tallahatchie.

A Song

JOSEPH BRODSKY

I wish you were here, dear,
I wish you were here.
I wish you sat on the sofa
and I sat near.
The handkerchief could be yours,
the tear could be mine, chin-bound.
Though it could be, of course,
the other way around.

I wish you were here, dear,
I wish you were here.
I wish we were in my car,
and you'd shift the gear.
We'd find ourselves elsewhere,
on an unknown shore.
Or else we'd repair
to where we've been before.

I wish you were here, dear,
I wish you were here.
I wish I knew no astronomy
when stars appear,
when the moon skims the water
that sighs and shifts in its slumber.
I wish it were still a quarter
to dial your number.

I wish you were here, dear,
in this hemisphere,

as I sit on the porch
sipping a beer.
It's evening, the sun is setting;
boys shout and gulls are crying.
What's the point of forgetting
if it's followed by dying?

Those Winter Sundays

ROBERT HAYDEN

Sundays too my father got up early
and put his clothes on in the blueblack cold,
then with cracked hands that ached
from labor in the weekday weather made
banked fires blaze. No one ever thanked him.

I'd wake and hear the cold splintering, breaking.
When the rooms were warm, he'd call,
and slowly I would rise and dress,
fearing the chronic angers of that house,

Speaking indifferently to him,
who had driven out the cold
and polished my good shoes as well.
What did I know, what did I know
of love's austere and lonely offices?

Asked for a Happy Memory of Her Father, She Recalls Wrigley Field

BETH ANN FENNELLY

His drinking was different in sunshine,
as if it couldn't be bad. Sudden, manic,
he swung into a laugh, bought me
two ice creams, said *One for each hand.*

Half the hot inning I licked Good Humor
running down wrists. My bird-mother
earlier, packing my pockets with sun block,
has hopped her warning: *Be careful.*

So, pinned between his knees, I held
his Old Style in both hands
while he streaked the lotion on my cheeks
and slurred *My little Indian princess.*

Home run: the hairy necks of men in front
jumped up, thighs torn from gummy green bleachers
to join the violent scramble. Father
held me close and said *Be careful,*

be careful. But why should I be full of care
with his thick arm circling my shoulders,
with a high smiling sun, like a home run,
in the upper right-hand corner of the sky?

forgiving my father

LUCILLE CLIFTON

it is friday. we have come
to the paying of the bills.
all week you have stood in my dreams
like a ghost, asking for more time
but today is payday, payday old man;
my mother's hand opens in her early grave
and i hold it out like a good daughter.

there is no more time for you. there will
never be time enough daddy daddy old lecher
old liar. i wish you were rich so i could take it all
and give the lady what she was due
but you were the son of a needy father,
the father of a needy son;
you gave her all you had
which was nothing, you have already given her
all you had.

you are the pocket that was going to open
and come up empty any friday.
you were each other's bad bargain, not mine.
daddy old pauper   old prisoner,   old dead man
what am i doing here collecting?
you lie side by side in debtors' boxes
and no accounting will open them up.

White Crane

DEAN YOUNG

I don't need to know any more about death
from the Japanese beetles
infesting the roses and plum
no matter what my neighbor sprays
in orange rubber gloves.
You can almost watch them writhe and wither,
pale and fall like party napkins
blown from a table just as light fades,
and the friends,
as often happens when light fades,
talk of something painful, glacial, pericardial,
and the napkins blow into the long grass.
When Basho writes of the long grass,
I don't need to know it has to do with death,
the characters reddish-brown and dim,
shadows of a rusted sword, an hour hand.
Imagine crossing mountains in summer snow
like Basho, all you own
on your back: brushes, robe,
the small gifts given in parting it's bad luck to leave behind.
I don't want to know what it's like to die on a rose,
sunk in perfume and fumes,
clutching,
to die in summer with everything off its knees,
daisies scattered like eyesight by the fence,
gladiolas open and fallen in mud,
weighed down with opening and breeze.
I wonder what your thoughts were, Father,

after they took your glasses and teeth,
all of us bunched around you like clouds
knocked loose of their moorings,
the white bird lying over you,
its beak down your throat.
Rain, heartbeats of rain.

Elegy

ARNOLD J. KEMP

for Paul Coppola (1966–1988)

It's too bad that Paul Coppola is dead
This morning. He and I could be listing
One-hundred flowers and their one-hundred
Mythological references. We could be
Walking over the same streets, restless,
Behind his big hotel or along the
Charles by a full moon that sits down on the
Bums sleeping near the rat's rippling trails
That cut across one-another as we wait
For dawn and a continental breakfast.
This morning I'm remembering the summer,
The waves on the great Lake Michigan,
Its small, sun-dried, silvery fish
Carcasses, grotesque husks that I didn't

Want to step on, the dust-tiny sea flies,
And the stench that faded in and out with
The tide on the only beach that I had
Ever walked on with my sister.
We were far away from home transfixed by
Those horizon-licking waves so strange in a lake.
There was a man straining his back and legs,
Pulling in a fish, and a woman,
A wrinkled sea artist, sat with her
Married daughter and captured it all with
A black line in her sketch book; another

Man was scaring his dachshund by dragging
It down to the stony edge of the beach,
Where the water was sucking and slurping.

cosmos, late blooming

D. A. POWELL

For Haines Eason

already the warm days taper to a plumate end: sky, where is your
      featherbed
some portion for me to fall to, in my contused and stricken state
not the extravagant robe I bartered for: tatters, pinked edges,
      unpressed

lord, I'm a homely child, scrabbling in the midden for my keep
why should you send this strapping gardener, hay in his teeth,
      to tend me
now that the showy crown begins to dip like a paper saucer

surely he'll not content with corrupted flesh that dismantles daily
so singular this closing act: spectacular ruin, the spark that descends
      in air
might he find no thrill in this trodden bower.   ragamuffin sum of
      veins

in my mouth the mausoleum of refusal: everything died inside me
including fish and vegetables, language and lovers, desire, yes, and
      passion
how could I make room in this crypt for another sorrow: caretaker:

lost man, these brambles part for your boots, denizened to my lot
your hand upon my stem now grasps the last shoots of summer
choose me for your chaplet, sweetheart.   wasted were my early
      flowers

Abiku

AFAA MICHAEL WEAVER

for Michael S. Weaver Jr. 1971–1972

The only way to chase ghosts is in the tub.
I close the bathroom door and let the room
fill with steam. My mind wiggles open.
I put music on my head to seal the world
inside me and flush out infecting spirits.
I touch hurt that is twenty-three years old,
the cold potato feel of your body in the coffin
like a toy. I touch the day I went mad with
grief at your fresh grave, see the night's sky
as I rode to Crownsville State Hospital.

If I had not fathered you before marriage,
if I had not thought you would make me a man,
if I had not forgotten children's suffering,
if I had not taken this road to madness,
what road would there have been for me?
Count my gifts to you—ten months of life,
my name engraved in bronze in the earth.

The Lost Pilot

JAMES TATE

for my father, 1922–1944

Your face did not rot
like the others—the co-pilot,
for example, I saw him

yesterday. His face is corn-
mush: his wife and daughter,
the poor ignorant people, stare

as if he will compose soon.
He was more wronged than Job.
But your face did not rot

like the others—it grew dark,
and hard like ebony;
the features progressed in their

distinction. If I could cajole
you to come back for an evening,
down from your compulsive

orbiting, I would touch you,
read your face as Dallas,
your hoodlum gunner, now,

with the blistered eyes, reads
his braille editions. I would
touch your face as a disinterested

scholar touches an original page.
However frightening, I would
discover you, and I would not

turn you in; I would not make
you face your wife, or Dallas,
or the co-pilot, Jim. You

could return to your crazy
orbiting, and I would not try
to fully understand what

it means to you. All I know
is this: when I see you,
as I have seen you at least

once every year of my life,
spin across the wilds of the sky
like a tiny, African god,

I feel dead. I feel as if I were
the residue of a stranger's life,
that I should pursue you.

My head cocked toward the sky,
I cannot get off the ground,
and, you, passing over again,

fast, perfect, and unwilling
to tell me that you are doing
well, or that it was mistake

that placed you in that world,
and me in this; or that misfortune
placed these worlds in us.

A Refusal to Mourn the Death, by Fire, of a Child in London

DYLAN THOMAS

Never until the mankind making
Bird beast and flower
Fathering and all humbling darkness
Tells with silence the last light breaking
And the still hour
Is come of the sea tumbling in harness

And I must enter again the round
Zion of the water bead
And the synagogue of the ear of corn
Shall I let pray the shadow of a sound
Or sow my salt seed
In the least valley of sackcloth to mourn

The majesty and burning of the child's death.
I shall not murder
The mankind of her going with a grave truth
Nor blaspheme down the stations of the breath
With any further
Elegy of innocence and youth.

Deep with the first dead lies London's daughter,
Robed in the long friends,
The grains beyond age, the dark veins of her mother,
Secret by the unmourning water
Of the riding Thames.
After the first death, there is no other.

Luke and the Duct Tape

COLEMAN BARKS

Nothing can save us. All this sweetness dies and rots.
Luke was a thirty-year-old pharmacy graduate
student who worked at Horton-Add Drugs,
at the post office in the back
that stays open until seven p.m., my post office.

It also has a lunch counter.
He sometimes did things behind there,
like make me a tuna fish sandwich
and fill a glass with ice and diet coke.

He mopped the place and swept up,
as quick and accurate with the broom-jabs
as he was at calculating my strange Tasmanian mail.
Hey, Finland! Once I sent out seventy-four books
priority mail. He said, It looked like Christmas
back there. In the storeroom where
the mailman picks up.

He laughed so easily with his quiet industry,
something out of Norman Rockwell.
He's maybe the most promising thing we are,
Luke, young American man just before
he meets a woman and raises a family
and does church group and Little League,
and every good thing stored in his strong hands
comes building out into the air.
Luke, master of small fixing.

Now on the glass double door, this handwritten
posterboard for his memorial service.
11 a.m. today. I missed it.
Would I have gone? *Luke Poucher.*
I never knew a last name.

One day we had some talk about how he knew
my name from all the mail, but I didn't know
his. Luke. That's a great name.

He was killed instantly last Thursday
in an automobile accident down the street
on Lumpkin at Old Princeton Road,
where he lived, not half a mile from me,
not a week ago. I had not heard
and don't now ask the Horton family for details.

Car wreck. Luke's dead. Luke 17:12.
The kingdom of God is within you.
He was so lightheartedly that,
it took your breath.

Is it with his death I fear my own
before the loving here gets as open
as it might could get in such as me?

I do not understand Dylan Thomas' "Refusal
to Mourn the Death of a Child
by Fire in London."

After the first death, there is no other,
he concludes, but on what authority?
He pictures his own death as entering
again the round Zion of the water bead . . .

the synagogue of the ear of corn,
and I have loved those words
since I first heard them in 1957.

I see the holy, tiny, elemental
corridors of corn grains and the fragile
tearshape inside the word *Zion.*
He says the nameless girl who burned
to death is now with the robed dead
by the unmourning Thames.

It may be Luke is off somewhere profound
and myriad, though I feel him close
and still-mortal as I write this, waiting
for the foolish satisfaction
of my own phrasing.

What is the sudden subtraction of a young man,
who might just as well be my son,
a filament of ocean beauty
I do and don't see today, do.

I grieve the death of Luke Poucher
for the place he swept and tended so well,
this fivepointed threshing floor
of stores and walkers and apartments,
mailmen, depositors, lunching retiree,
chemo-waver, body-worker, skateboarder,
UPS, any bunch that knows each other's
half-grin in hurried irritation
out doing errands.

Let this be Luke, this end of the parking lot
around the mailboxes, Luke Poucher Place.

The air, the few flowers,
and the people as they meet going in
to buy lunch or stamps or shampoo,
their small nods of helplessness.

I asked for duct tape once.
*You know, we ought to carry that,
but we don't.* It's about all I know
how to do to fix anything.

I've got some broken ducks.
I need to get them in a row.

Let this low talking, the love and joking
we do fumbling for courtesy
here at the door be Luke, Luke
looking up from the stroke
of his all-hallowing broom, *Beautiful
out there, idn't it?*

Birthday Poem

ERIN MURPHY

It's 2 a.m. and I can't remember
the last name of my friend Joy
who died of breast cancer.
I can see her wig, slightly matted,
with the curls she always wanted,
see her holding hands with her daughter
that afternoon we walked to Long Point.
But the name . . . a *W*, I think . . . damn it . . .
Joy, who kicked her drinking husband out
the last month, who interviewed
the local politician (*no sir, tell me*
what you think, not what you think
everyone wants you to think),
who drew a thousand yellow smiley faces
and called it *Portraits of Prozac*.
Walton? Williams? Winston?
I brought her copies of *Vanity Fair* and *People*,
heated a few cans of tomato soup
in her grease-splattered kitchen.
I never took an SOS pad to that back-splash
or made a homemade stew, never
drove her, like her good neighbor did,
to the Grand Canyon, i.v. trolley in tow.
I just sat with her every few weeks
in that dark bedroom that smelled
of her daughter's new kittens,
picked up her spilled blue pills
from the carpet under her bed and ticked them

one by one into the bottle,
reaching for them the way I'm combing my mind
now for her name: Wilson? Wiggins?
The tattered paisley address book
is gone so I can't look her up
and anyone who knew her is asleep now
so I can't call—and besides,
my stepdaughter is downstairs talking
to a boyfriend an ocean away,
which is how far I feel from late-night
hushed giggles and a phone cord
stretched to the front stoop,
that is how old I am now, old enough
to have forgotten the name of a friend
who died, *died* for God's sake,
not a friend who gave me a ride
to Syracuse one weekend or loaned me
a gown for a college ball.
Her daughter lives with the ex now.
He's remarried and sober, I'm told.
Once when my husband and son
ran out of gas on Route 213,
the new wife picked them up in her red Saab
and took them to the Texaco in Galena.
She seems nice, they said. Dyes her hair.
Gwinner. Joy Gwinner. And her daughter's name
is Hope.

You Don't Miss Your Water

CORNELIUS EADY

At home, my mother wakes up and spends some of her day talking back to my father's empty chair.

In Florida, my sister experiences the occasional dream in which my father returns; they chat.

He's been dead and gone for a little over a year. How it would please me to hear his unrecorded voice again, now alive only in the minds of those who remember him.

If I could, if as in the old spiritual, I could actually get a direct phone link to the other side, I could call him up, tell him about this small prize of a week I've had teaching poetry at a ski resort a few miles from Lake Tahoe, imagination jackpot, brief paradise of letters.

How could I make him believe that I have gotten all of this, this modern apartment, this pond in front of my window, all from the writing of a few good lines of verse, my father, who distrusted anything he couldn't get his hands on?

Most likely, he would listen, then ask me, as he always did, just for safety's sake, if my wife still had her good-paying job.

And I can't tell you why, but this afternoon, I wouldn't become hot and stuffy from his concern, think "old fool," and gripe back, *Of course I'm still teaching college. It's summer, you know?*

This afternoon, I miss his difficult waters. And when he'd ask, as he always would, *How're they treating you?* I'd love to answer back, *Fine, daddy. They're paying me to write about your life.*

The Dead

BILLY COLLINS

The dead are always looking down on us, they say,
while we are putting on our shoes or making a sandwich,
they are looking down through the glass-bottom boats of heaven
as they row themselves slowly through eternity.

They watch the tops of our heads moving below on earth,
and when we lie down in a field or on a couch,
drugged perhaps by the hum of a warm afternoon,
they think we are looking back at them,

which makes them lift their oars and fall silent
and wait, like parents, for us to close our eyes.

IV.
Ritual

Tomorrow, the bowl I have yet to fill.
—NATASHA TRETHEWEY

Water

PHILIP LARKIN

If I were called in
To construct a religion
I should make use of water.

Going to church
Would entail a fording
To dry, different clothes;

My liturgy would employ
Images of sousing,
A furious devout drench,

And I should raise in the east
A glass of water
Where any-angled light
Would congregate endlessly.

My Religion

ANNE CARSON

My religion makes no sense
and does not help me
therefore I pursue it.

When we see
how simple it would have been
we will thrash ourselves.

I had a vision
of all the people in the world
who are searching for God

massed in a room
on one side
of a partition

that looks
from the other side
(God's side)

transparent
but we are blind.
Our gestures are blind.

Our blind gestures continue
for some time until finally
from somewhere

on the other side of the partition there we are
looking back at them.
It is far too late.

We see how brokenly
how warily
how ill

our blind gestures
parodied
what God really wanted

(some simple thing).
The thought of it
(this simple thing)

is like a creature
let loose in a room
and battering

to get out.
It batters my soul
with its rifle butt.

The Truth the Dead Know

ANNE SEXTON

For my mother, born March 1902, died March 1959
and my father, born February 1900, died June 1959

Gone, I say and walk from church,
refusing the stiff procession to the grave,
letting the dead ride alone in the hearse.
It is June. I am tired of being brave.

We drive to the Cape. I cultivate
myself where the sun gutters from the sky,
where the sea swings in like an iron gate
and we touch. In another country people die.

My darling, the wind falls in like stones
from the whitehearted water and when we touch
we enter touch entirely. No one's alone.
Men kill for this, or for as much.

And what of the dead? They lie without shoes
in their stone boats. They are more like stone
than the sea would be if it stopped. They refuse
to be blessed, throat, eye and knucklebone.

Listen Lord: A Prayer

JAMES WELDON JOHNSON

O Lord, we come this morning
Knee-bowed and body-bent
Before thy throne of grace.
O Lord—this morning—
Bow our hearts beneath our knees,
And our knees in some lonesome valley.
We come this morning—
Like empty pitchers to a full fountain,
With no merits of our own.
O Lord—open up a window of heaven,
And lean out far over the battlements of glory,
And listen this morning.

Lord, have mercy on proud and dying sinners—
Sinners hanging over the mouth of hell,
Who seem to love their distance well.
Lord—ride by this morning—
Mount your milk-white horse,
And ride-a this morning—
And in your ride, ride by old hell,
Ride by the dingy gates of hell,
And stop poor sinners in their headlong plunge.

And now, O Lord, this man of God,
Who breaks the bread of life this morning—
Shadow him in the hollow of thy hand,
And keep him out of the gunshot of the devil.
Take him, Lord—this morning—

Wash him with hyssop inside and out,
Hang him up and drain him dry of sin.
Pin his ear to the wisdom-post,
And make his words sledge hammers of truth—
Beating on the iron heart of sin.
Lord God, this morning—
Put his eye to the telescope of eternity,
And let him look upon the paper walls of time.
Lord, turpentine his imagination,
Put perpetual motion in his arms,
Fill him full of the dynamite of thy power,
Anoint him all over with the oil of thy salvation,
And set his tongue on fire.

And now, O Lord—
When I've done drunk my last cup of sorrow—
When I've been called everything but a child of God—
When I'm done travelling up the rough side of the mountain—
O—Mary's Baby—
When I start down the steep and slippery steps of death—
When this old world begins to rock beneath my feet—
Lower me to my dusty grave in peace
To wait for that great gittin' up morning—Amen.

Dedication for a Plot of Ground

WILLIAM CARLOS WILLIAMS

This plot of ground
facing the waters of this inlet
is dedicated to the living presence of
Emily Dickinson Wellcome
who was born in England; married;
lost her husband and with
her five year old son
sailed for New York in a two-master;
was driven to the Azores;
ran adrift on Fire Island shoal,
met her second husband
in a Brooklyn boarding house,
went with him to Puerto Rico
bore three more children, lost
her second husband, lived hard
for eight years in St. Thomas,
Puerto Rico, San Domingo, followed
the oldest son to New York,
lost her daughter, lost her "baby,"
seized the two boys of
the oldest son by the second marriage
mothered them—they being
motherless—fought for them
against the other grandmother
and the aunts, brought them here
summer after summer, defended
herself here against thieves,
storms, sun, fire,

against flies, against girls
that came smelling about, against
drought, against weeds, storm-tides,
neighbors, weasels that stole her chickens,
against the weakness of her own hands,
against the growing strength of
the boys, against wind, against
the stones, against trespassers,
against rents, against her own mind.

She grubbed this earth with her own hands,
domineered over this grass plot,
blackguarded her oldest son
into buying it, lived here fifteen years,
attained a final loneliness and—

If you can bring nothing to this place
but your carcass, keep out.

Facing It

YUSEF KOMUNYAKAA

My black face fades,
hiding inside the black granite.
I said I wouldn't,
dammit: No tears.
I'm stone. I'm flesh.
My clouded reflection eyes me
like a bird of prey, the profile of night
slanted against morning. I turn
this way—the stone lets me go.
I turn that way—I'm inside
the Vietnam Veterans Memorial
again, depending on the light
to make a difference.
I go down the 58,022 names,
half-expecting to find
my own in letters like smoke.
I touch the name Andrew Johnson;
I see the booby trap's white flash.
Names shimmer on a woman's blouse
but when she walks away
the names stay on the wall.
Brushstrokes flash, a red bird's
wings cutting across my stare.
The sky. A plane in the sky.
A white vet's image floats
closer to me, then his pale eyes
look through mine. I'm a window.
He's lost his right arm

inside the stone. In the black mirror
a woman's trying to erase names:
No, she's brushing a boy's hair.

Funeral Rites

SEAMUS HEANEY

I

I shouldered a kind of manhood
stepping in to lift the coffins
of dead relations.
They had been laid out

in tainted rooms,
their eyelids glistening,
their dough-white hands
shackled in rosary beads.

Their puffed knuckles
had unwrinkled, the nails
were darkened, the wrists
obediently sloped.

The dulse-brown shroud,
the quilted satin cribs:
I knelt courteously
admiring it all

as wax melted down
and veined the candles,
the flames hovering
to the women hovering

behind me.
And always, in a corner,

the coffin lid,
its nail-heads dressed

with little gleaming crosses.
Dear soapstone masks,
kissing their igloo brows
had to suffice

before the nails were sunk
and the black glacier
of each funeral
pushed away.

II

Now as news comes in
of each neighbourly murder
we pine for ceremony,
customary rhythms:

the temperate footsteps
of a cortège, winding past
each blinded home.
I would restore

the great chambers of Boyne,
prepare a sepulchre
under the cupmarked stones.
Out of side-streets and by-roads

purring family cars
nose into line,
the whole country tunes
to the muffled drumming

of ten thousand engines.
Somnambulant women,
left behind, move
through emptied kitchens

imagining our slow triumph
towards the mounds.
Quiet as a serpent
in its grassy boulevard,

the procession drags its tail
out of the Gap of the North
as its head already enters
the megalithic doorway.

III

When they have put the stone
back in its mouth
we will drive north again
past Strang and Carling fjords,

the cud of memory
allayed for once, arbitration
of the feud placated,
imagining those under the hill

disposed like Gunnar
who lay beautiful
inside his burial mound,
though dead by violence

and unavenged.
Men said that he was chanting

verses about honour
and that four lights burned

in corners of the chamber:
which opened then, as he turned
with a joyful face
to look at the moon.

Not Forgotten

TOI DERRICOTTE

I love the way the black ants use their dead.
They carry them off like warriors on their steel
backs. They spend hours struggling, lifting,
dragging, so that even the dead will be of service.
It is not grisly—as it would be for us—
to carry them back to be eaten. I think of
my husband at his father's grave—
the grass had closed
over the headstone and the name had disappeared. He took out
a pocket knife and cut the grass away; he swept it
with his handkerchief to make it clear. "Is this the way
we'll be forgotten?" And he bent down over the grave and wept.

After Your Death

NATASHA TRETHEWEY

First, I emptied the closets of your clothes,
threw out the bowl of fruit, bruised
from your touch, left empty the jars

you bought for preserves. The next morning,
birds rustled the fruit trees, and later
when I twisted a ripe fig loose from its stem,

I found it half eaten, the other side
already rotting, or—like another I plucked
and split open—being taken from the inside:

a swarm of insects hollowing it. I'm too late,
again, another space emptied by loss.
Tomorrow, the bowl I have yet to fill.

Disposal

W. D. SNODGRASS

The unworn long gown, meant for dances
She would have scarcely dared attend,
Is fobbed off on a friend—
Who can't help wondering if it's spoiled
But thinks, well, she can take her chances.

We roll her spoons up like old plans
Or failed securities, seal their case,
Then lay them back. One lace
Nightthing lies in the chest, unsoiled
By wear, untouched by human hands.

We don't dare burn those cancelled patterns
And markdowns that she actually wore,
Yet who do we know so poor
They'd take them? Spared all need, all passion,
Saved from loss, she lies boxed in satins

Like a pair of party shoes
That seemed to never find a taker;
We send back to its maker
A life somehow gone out of fashion
But still too good to use.

Seersucker Suit

DEBORAH DIGGES

To the curator of the museum, to the exhibition of fathers,
to the next room from this closet of trousers
and trousers, full sail the walnut hangers of shirts,
O the great ghost ships of his shoes.
Through the racks and the riggings,
belt buckles ringing and coins in coat pockets
and moths that fly up from the black woolen remnants,
his smell like a kiss blown through hallways of cedar,
the shape of him locked in his burial clothes,
his voice tucked deep in his name,
his keys and the bells to his heart,
I am passing his light blue seersucker suit
with one grass-stained knee,
and a white shirt, clean boxers, clean socks, a handkerchief.

Until She Returns

REGINALD SHEPHERD

This is how I say it ends, Bronx County, 1978.
Packed up all my cares and woe in a plastic
garbage bag. It took an hour, maybe
less.
    I take myself into the river of salt
for pages at a time, lying for the sake of
accuracy. All that summer it was winter; I said it
for her sake.
                (For a year after she died
I dreamed of her; she came to say
she was just hiding. Death was just
a place to stay, a drift of cloud smeared half-way into
snow. I watched it fall.) (It never snowed there,
pine needles on red clay and heat-reek of the paper mill
for months. Mere decor, you might say, caves of kudzu
and no sidewalks. I missed sidewalks
most of all.) Some Thursday's drift of cloud stole forty years
in passing, and an extra for good luck. Some other spring
I'll give them back.
                Days spent
curled around a tattered name, erased: white
piss-smelling flowers, intimate
spring air against the throat, some warmth
not far enough away. My little sister said
we'll have to find another . . . ; we were named
after each other, before the fact. Who isn't her these days?
Hat boxes and a closet full of coats with fur collars,
someone to betray over and over. (The personal effects

incinerated, with no one to say
mine. I'll take the rhinestone buckles on the shoes.)

When death comes he'll be a fine young man
and I will kiss his rotten lips and find her there.
Here I go, singing low.

the oboe in Handel's largo
from *Xerxes* as elegy

QUAN BARRY

Put what will be your tongue in a glass of warm water. Let it soften, the
    reed's clean wood smooth & expanding.

At that age I never believed I could make anything beautiful.

& then I did.

How w/practice I was able to pin paper to the wall using only my
    breath, vibrato controlled as a hummingbird.

This is the fingers' work, the long notes like eggs on the page.

How in our second season both your parents died though I still looked
    for them gaunt & ligneous on the stoop, their frail hands
    pianissimo & waving.

Through the oboe I came to know things: dolce & sorrow, why an
    aragonaise is like a blue flame dancing, or how an adagio is
    sheened like moonrise.

Sweetness & affliction.

Then Mr. Harlick lifted his baton & we took our instruments up in our
    hands—the largo's non-narrative suffering

like an oak tree, something I could climb.

Who am I to have everything?

All I could do was take the reed from the water & push it into pitch.
Purse my lips. Come in like light growing.

Transaction

A. R. AMMONS

I attended the burial of all my rosy feelings:
I performed the rites, simple and decisive:
the long box took the spilling of gray ground in
with little evidence of note: I traded slow

work for the usual grief: the services were private:
there was little cause for show, though no cause not
to show: it went indifferently, with an appropriate
gravity and lack of noise: the ceremonies of the self

seem always to occur at a distance from the ruins of men
where there is nothing really much to expect, no arms,
no embraces: the day was all right: certain occasions
outweigh the weather: the woods just to the left

were average woods: well, I turned around finally from
the process, the surface smoothed into a kind of seal,
and tried to notice what might be thought to remain:
everything was there, the sun, the breeze, the woods

(as I said), the little mound of troublesome tufts of
grass: but the trees were upright shadows, the breeze
was as against a shade, the woods stirred gray
as deep water: I looked around for what was left,

the tools, and took them up and went away, leaving
all my treasures where they might never again disturb
me, increase or craze: decision quietens:
shadows are bodiless shapes, yet they have a song.

My Father's Body

WILLIAM MATTHEWS

First they take it away,
for now the body belongs to the state.
Then they open it
to see what may have killed it,
and the body had arteriosclerosis
in its heart, for this was an inside job.
Now someone must identify the body
so that the state may have a name
for what it will give away,
and the funeral people come in a stark car
shaped like a coffin with a hood
and take the body away,
for now it belongs to the funeral people
and the body's family buys it back,
though it lies in a box at the crematorium
while the mourners travel and convene.
Then they bring the body to the chapel, as they call it,
of the crematorium, and the body lies in its box
while the mourners enter and sit
and stare at the box, for the box
lies on a pedestal where the altar would be
if this were a chapel.
A rectangular frame with curtains at the sides
rises from the pedestal,
so that the box seems to fill a small stage,
and the stage gives off the familiar
illusion of being a box with one wall torn away
so that we may see into it,

but it's filled with a box we can't see into.
There's music on tape and a man in a robe
speaks for a while and I speak
for a while and then there's a prayer
and then we mourners can hear the whir
of a small motor and curtains slide
across the stage. At least for today,
I think, this is the stage that all the world is,
and another motor hums on
and we mourners realize that behind
the curtains the body is being lowered,
not like Don Giovanni to the flames
but without flourish or song
or the comforts of elaborate plot,
to the basement of the crematorium,
to the mercies of the gas jets
and the balm of the conveyer belt.
The ashes will be scattered,
says a hushed man in a mute suit,
in the Garden of Remembrance,
which is out back.
And what's left of a mild, democratic man
will sift in a heap with the residue of others,
for now they all belong to time.

My Mother's Body, My Professor, My Bower

JEAN VALENTINE

Who died? My mother's body,
my professor, my bower,
my giant clam.
Serene water, professor
of copious clay,
of spiraling finger-holes in the clay,
of blue breast-milk,
first pulse, all thought:
there is nothing to get. You can't eat money,
dear throat, dear longing,
dear belly, dear fatness,
dear silky fastness: ecstatic lungs' breath,
you can't protect yourself,
there is nothing to get.

Dead Letters

MARY JO SALTER

I.

Dear Mrs. Salter: Congratulations! You
(no need to read on—yet I always do)
may have won the sweepstakes, if you'll send . . .
Is this how it must end?
Or will it ever end? The bills, all paid,
come monthly anyway, to cheer the dead.
BALANCE: decimal point and double o's
like pennies no one placed upon your eyes.
I never saw you dead—you simply vanished,
your body gone to Science, as you wished:
I was the one to send you there, by phone,
on that stunned morning answering the blunt
young nurse who called, wanting to "clear the room."
"Take her," I said, "I won't be coming in"—
couldn't bear to see your cherished face with more
death in it than was there five days before.
But now, where are you really? From the mail
today, it seems, you might almost be well:
Dear Patient: It's been three years since your eyes
were checked . . . A host of worthy causes vies
for your attention: endangered wildlife funds,
orphans with empty bowls in outstretched hands,
political prisoners, Congressmen. The *LAST*
*ISSUE*s of magazines are never last.
And now you've shored up on some realtors' list,
since word went out you've "moved" to my address:
Dear New Apartment Owner: If you rent . . .

Mother, in daydreams sometimes I am sent
to follow you, my own forwarding text
Dear Mrs. Salter's Daughter: You are next.

II.

When I try to concentrate
on who you were,
images of you blur
and pulsate, like the clothes
left in your closet—

every size from four to fourteen,
not progressively,
but back and forth again:
testaments to Treatment
after Treatment.

Injected, radiated,
bloated, balded, nauseated;
years in an iron wig that ill
fit or befitted you;
then more years, unexpected,

of a cobweb gray you grew
in thanks to covet:
lurching from reprieve to reprieve,
you taught yourself to live
with less and less,

and so did we—
even, at last, without the giddy
vastness of your love,
so painfully withdrawn when pain
became all you could think of.

Trying not to feel
that nothing, not even love
or death, is original,
like other mourners I've
turned up happy photographs—

of the ruby-lipsticked girl
(in black-and-white, but I can tell)
on your wedding day; or, here, a scene
in a hallway I'd hardly know was ours
but for that gilt barometer.

Had I lost that about you?
Your regal touch—china in green
and gold; silk Oriental dresses?
. . . Days that made you queen
of nothing but your high-backed bed

convinced you
you'd been singled out to die.
Yet here you are,
a smiling hostess at the door
bidding your friends goodbye:

What blessedness!
—To think that once
you hadn't had to be the focus,
could go on living unpitied,
even unnoticed.

III.

Dinner in Boston. I am twenty-three,
and you have come to see
your grown-up daughter in her element.

My choice is cheap and almost elegant:
crêpes and spinach salad, a carafe
of chilled house wine we laugh

companionably over. Memory drifts
back to well-set tables shared at home—
those animated dinners you would chair
(the Salter Seminars, my boyfriend called them)
where you taught me to admire
the complex givens of your gifts

for life. Accomplished cook,
stickler for decorum, you liked to shock
us with the heedless, vocal sweep
of your opinions: on the Catholic Church
(you hate it, so you think—hate it so much
you'll find a slow way back);

the saintliness of Adlai; Armageddon.
(Once, you greeted me from school with news
the Chinese had invaded us: a thrill
that never found its way to print,
but you shrugged off my complaint:
"If they haven't done it yet, you know they will.")

Tonight, Newbury Street—
scene of my happy lunch hours, of the young
executives with ice cream cones
dripping down their hands, bright students in new jeans—
outside our window takes, as night sifts down,
that memorializing cast of light

you seem to shed on things, all by yourself.
Even when all is well (the illness
more under control than less,

you're devoting all your time to sculpture
bigger than you are—filling every shelf
in the garage!) I still recapture

moments before they're over.
She loved me so, that when I praised her shirt
she took it off her back, or
We drank four cups of tea apiece . . . Alert
always to what perishes, I invert
your low, confiding chuckle now and pour

its darkness like a stain across our table.
"Can you remember Grandma's laugh? I can't,"
I interrupt, and having voiced the fear,
immediately am able:
it sounded like a baby's xylophone,
thrown down a flight of stairs.

Who could have forgotten *that*?
I laugh myself—but now I've spoiled
the mood, or turned it oversweet,
and you reach into your magic purse
for a snapshot of your mother. "Here, it's yours."
Stunned how soon my eyes have filled

with tears—how easy it has been
to give a pleasing answer—
you seem relieved to put to death
a momentary fright not only mine.
Now, your own forever-
unrecorded voice cut short by cancer,

I still find myself asking: dear
as she was, didn't you know
it's you I was crying for?

IV.

We're on our way to the hospital
for the twenty-thousandth time.
You used to drive—then I;
lately, we've piled into a taxi.
Each week a new man takes the rap
for bumps and jolts; if not for him
(you imply) we'd have a pleasant trip.
Shrunken and old, collapsible,
head in my lap, you start up in alarm:
"Mary Jo—I think I'm ill."

Forgive me that I laughed!
It's too late to apologize;
but that you could find it in you still
to register surprise—
that *you'd* hope to be well . . .
It kept you alive, of course,
those years of asking visitors
"Are your ears ringing?" as if there might
someday be found a blanket cause
for pains that kept you up all night.

V.

If you could see your daughter, no green thumb,
tending the philodendron
you sent me when my baby girl was born!
If you could see my daughter: that refrain
twists like a crimping weed, a vine of pain
around the joy of everything she learns.

And yet it intertwines
forever, I perceive, your life and mine.
From time to time, a heart-shaped leaf will turn

yellow and fall—in falling a leaf torn
out of your life again,
the story I must constantly revive.

I water it and live;
water and wait for other plants to bloom.
I took them from your room
nearly a year ago now, poinsettias
of that wizened, stricken Christmas
you floated through five days before the end.

One's inky-red; the other paper-white . . .
You too were one to note
life's artful correspondences.
But I can't let them go,
not yet; and granted time to tend
a growing tenderness, I send

more letters, Mother—these despite
the answers you can't write.

"I needed to talk to my sister"

GRACE PALEY

I needed to talk to my sister
talk to her on the telephone   I mean
just as I used to every morning
in the evening too whenever the
grandchildren said a sentence that
clasped both our hearts

I called   her phone rang four times
you can imagine my breath stopped   then
there was a terrible telephonic noise
a voice said   this number is no
longer in use   how wonderful I
thought   I can
call again they have not yet assigned
her number to another person despite
two years of absence due to death

Fatal April

THOMAS SAYERS ELLIS

Thomas Leon Ellis Sr. (1945–1991)

The phone rang. It was Doris,
Your sister, calling to say
April had taken you, where,
In your bedroom, when, days ago,
How, murder, no a stroke.

You left a car (but I
Don't drive) and enough cash
In your pockets to buy
A one-way train ticket
From Boston to Washington.

Let's get one thing straight.
I didn't take the money, but
I did take your driver's license
And the Chuck Brown album,
Needle-to-groove,

Round and round,
Where they found you.
Both were metaphors:
The license (I promised, but knew
I'd never get, now I have yours)

And the album because
Of what you may have been
Trying to say about writing,

About home. James keeps
Asking me to visit your grave,

When will I learn to drive
And why I changed my name.
He's your son, stubborn with
An inherited temper. I keep telling him
No, never, there's more than

One way to bury a man.

Celestial Music

LOUISE GLÜCK

I have a friend who still believes in heaven.
Not a stupid person, yet with all she knows, she literally talks to god,
she thinks someone listens in heaven.
On earth, she's unusually competent.
Brave, too, able to face unpleasantness.

We found a caterpillar dying in the dirt, greedy ants crawling over it.
I'm always moved by weakness, by disaster, always eager to oppose
        vitality.
But timid, also, quick to shut my eyes.
Whereas my friend was able to watch, to let events play out
according to nature. For my sake, she intervened,
brushing a few ants off the torn thing, and set it down across the road.

My friend says I shut my eyes to god, that nothing else explains
my aversion to reality. She says I'm like the child who buries her head
        in the pillow
so as not to see, the child who tells herself
that light causes sadness—
My friend is like the mother. Patient, urging me
to wake up an adult like herself, a courageous person—

In my dreams, my friend reproaches me. We're walking
on the same road, except it's winter now;
she's telling me that when you love the world you hear celestial music:
look up, she says. When I look up, nothing.
Only clouds, snow, a white business in the trees
like brides leaping to a great height—

Then I'm afraid for her; I see her
caught in a net deliberately cast over the earth—

In reality, we sit by the side of the road, watching the sun set;
from time to time, the silence pierced by a birdcall.
It's this moment we're both trying to explain, the fact
that we're at ease with death, with solitude.
My friend draws a circle in the dirt; inside, the caterpillar doesn't
          move.
She's always trying to make something whole, something beautiful,
          an image
capable of life apart from her.
We're very quiet. It's peaceful sitting here, not speaking, the
          composition
fixed, the road turning suddenly dark, the air
going cool, here and there the rocks shining and glittering—
it's this stillness that we both love.
The love of form is a love of endings.

God

MICHAEL RYAN

for D. B.

Maybe you're a verb, or some
lost part of speech
that would let us talk sense
instead of monkey-screech

when we try to explain you
to our loved ones and ourselves
when we most need to.
Who knows why someone dies

in the thick of happiness,
his true love finally found,
the world showering success
as if the world were only a cloud

that floated in a dream
above a perfect day?
Are you also dreaming our words?
Give us something to say.

Trying to Pray

JAMES WRIGHT

This time, I have left my body behind me, crying
In its dark thorns.
Still,
There are good things in this world.
It is dusk.
It is the good darkness
Of women's hands that touch loaves.
The spirit of a tree begins to move.
I touch leaves.
I close my eyes, and think of water.

Ice Storm

ROBERT HAYDEN

Unable to sleep, or pray, I stand
by the window looking out
at moonstruck trees a December storm
has bowed with ice.

Maple and mountain ash bend
under its glassy weight,
their cracked branches falling upon
the frozen snow.

The trees themselves, as in winters past,
will survive their burdening,
broken thrive. And am I less to You,
my God, than they?

Wasteful Gesture Only Not

TONY HOAGLAND

Ruth visits her mother's grave in the California hills.
She knows her mother isn't there but the rectangle of grass
marks off the place where the memories are kept,

like a library book named *Dorothy*.
Some of the chapters might be: *Dorothy:*
Better Bird-Watcher Than Cook;

Dorothy, Wife and Atheist;
Passionate Recycler Dorothy. Here Lies But Not.
In the summer hills, where the tall tough grass

reminds you of persistence
and the endless wind
reminds you of indifference,

Ruth brings batches of white roses,
extravagant gesture not entirely wasteful
because as soon as she is gone she knows
the deer come out of the woods to eat them.

What was made for the eye
goes into the mouth,
thinks Ruth to herself as she drives away,
and in bed when she tries to remember her mother,

she drifts instead to the roses,
and when she thinks about the roses she
sees instead the deer chewing them—

the pale petals of the roses in the dark
warm bellies of the sleeping deer—
that's what going to sleep is like.

Blues Procession

TERRANCE HAYES

for Uncle Bubba (1953–1985)

Come tomorrow, our car had to be bright
As the preacher's capped teeth.

They'd found my uncle's car bundled
In the arms of a tree;

The gin bottle & windshield cracked,
The flesh like moss clinging to his body . . .

My mother knelt with rag & bucket
To knuckle insects from the grill,

I did not know the detours of grief.
I did not know the detours from grief.

I watched her curse untangling the hose
Noosed around her feet I watched suds

Slide down the glass like storm clouds
Bound to wreck her somewhere in the week.

I Just Wanna Testify

CORNELIUS EADY

There was, at the end, a look of great peace on my father's face at the moment of his death. At the memorial service my cousin tells this story to us as a way to infer a last-minute salvation, a meeting of Jesus in the middle of the air, this being, after all, the AME Zionist church across from the vacant lot that used to be the elementary school me and my sister attended.

This is the part of the service where we stand up for him, this small knot of family and friends in a very large room.

He's gone and left my mother with nothing. Her name isn't on the deed to the house, her name never appears on his policies. Her mind's confused, she can't take care of herself by herself, and I'm having a real hard time convincing various agencies that she even exists.

Which is why there is no casket to bear. Too expensive, we decide, money to be better spent on the living, on my mother.

Still, we give him a family send-off. *A hard man, but his own man!* Sing the testimonies. *A stingy man, but a family man!* And I truthfully thank him for the roof he put over our heads, for staying when a lot of other men took a look at their wives, their babies, their house bills and changed their names to fare-thee-well.

And then my sister stands up, stands up through the pain and accidents of first born, first torn, stands up, the family's "bad girl," the willful daughter, low-down spirit of red dresses and iodine, my sister stands up in a way I can't fully explain, but know belongs to black women, she stands up and declares, *I'm just like him, but I'm a woman, so I can't get away with it.*

Incensation at the Funeral

MATTHEW ROHRER

May the angels lead you into paradise
which is your love affair with the plump old woman.

May the martyrs lead you, joyous couple, into the holy city,

where it is still and the trees touching the dark sky are burdened.
After the rain they are still burdened.

May the Innocents save you a campsite in the woods north of the
      holy city,
with the mist falling from the pines
with the stars' electricity.

May the prophets let you tinker at their toolbenches.
May there be chocolate.
May there be no almonds.

May the diggers have the dirt hidden when we come to the grave.

May the work be made easy for us. May they have the device.
You would love the device.

My Father's Funeral

KARL SHAPIRO

Lurching from gloomy limousines we slip
On the warm baby-blanket of Baltimore snow,
Wet flakes smacking our faces like distraught
Kisses on cheeks, and step upon the green
Carpet of artificial grass which crunches
Underfoot, as if it were eating, and come
To the canopy, a half-shelter which provides
A kind of room to enclose us all, and the hole,
And the camp chairs, and following after,
The scrolly walnut coffin
That has my father in it.

Minutes ago in the noncommittal chapel
I saw his face, not looking himself at all
In that compartment hinged to open and shut,
A vaudeville prop with a small waxen man,
"So cold," the widow said and shied away
In a wide arc of centrifugal motion,
To come again to stand like me beside,
In the flowerless room with electric candelabra.
If there is among our people any heaven,
We are rather ambiguous about it
And tend to ignore the subject.

The rabbi's eulogy is succinct,
Accurate and sincere, and the great prayer
That finishes the speech is simply praise
Of God, the god my father took in stride

When he made us learn Hebrew and shorthand,
Taught us to be superior, as befits
A nation of individual priests.
At my sister's house we neither pray nor cry
Nor sit, but stand and drink and joke,
So that one of the youngsters says
It's more like a cocktail party.

For Dylan's dandy villanelle,
For Sylvia's oath of damnation one reserves
A technical respect. To Miller's Willie
And Lewis's Babbitt I demur.
My father was writing a book on salesmanship
While he was dying; it was his book of poems,
Destined to be unpublished. He hadn't time
To master books but kept the house well stocked
With random volumes, like a ship's library,
Rows and rows of forgotten classics,
Books for the sake of having books.

My father in black knee-socks and high shoes
Holding a whip to whip a top upstreet;
My father the court stenographer,
My father in slouch hat in the Rockies,
My father kissing my mother,
My father kissing his secretary,
In the high-school yearbook captioned Yid,
In synagogue at six in the morning praying
Three hundred and sixty-five days for his mother's rest,
My father at my elbow on the bimah
And presiding over the Sabbath.

In the old forgotten purlieus of the city
A Jewish ghetto in its day, there lie

My father's father, mother and the rest,
Now only a ghetto lost to time,
Ungreen, unwhite, unterraced like the new
Cemetery to which my father goes.
Abaddon, the old place of destruction;
Sheol, a new-made garden of the dead
Under the snow. Shalom be to his life,
Shalom be to his death.

Cold Calls

EDWARD HIRSCH

If you had watched my father,
who had been peddling boxes for fifty years,
working the phones again at a common desk,

if you had listened to him sweet-talking
the newly minted assistant buyer at Seagram's

and swearing a little under his breath,

if you had sweated with him on the docks
of a medical supply company
and heard him boasting, as I did,
that he had to kiss some strange asses,

if you had seen him dying out there,

then you would understand why I stood
at his grave on those wintry afternoons
and stared at the bare muddy trees

and raved in silence to no one,
to his name carved into a granite slab.

Cold calls, dead accounts.

Burial [No Woman No Cry]

KEVIN YOUNG

We circle the grave
in dark coats like buzzards.
The men, me too, this morning
had lifted you, steering

your wooden ship through
metal doors to the living room.
I couldn't stand to see
the screws still loose.

A plank it felt we walked.
They lifted the lid
right there and we filed
past like ants, bearing

twice our weight
in sorrow. It wasn't
true. That ain't you—
too grey, and serious,

right side of your face
fallen, cotton
filling your nose—
at least the suit looked new.

We held each other a long time
after and could not speak,
like you. Get up,
Stand up, we'll sing

later, the reggae you loved
your brother will strum
stumbling on a guitar, and for
a moment you'll be there, here,

where we'd been brought to visit
too late, like fools.
At the grave we step
past crumbling stones

and dead flowers to stand
on the red rise
of dirt already dug
for you. The sound

of them letting you down.
The sound of men scraping
and scraping what
I can't quite see, spreading

the cool concrete
over you by hand. And it takes
long, so long, like death—
like we once thought life.

The choir lifts us up
with their voices above
the coconut trees—*Habari
Jemba* they sing—

and the tune tells me Isn't That
Good News.
Cell phones chiming
their songs too.

After, we place white flowers
on your hardening tomb.
Is it only the sun
we shade our faces from?

Our sweat a thousand tears.

Mourners

TED KOOSER

After the funeral, the mourners gather
under the rustling churchyard maples
and talk softly, like clusters of leaves.
White shirt cuffs and collars flash in the shade:
highlights on deep green water.
They came this afternoon to say goodbye,
but now they keep saying hello and hello,
peering into each other's faces,
slow to let go of each other's hands.

Lament

LOUISE GLÜCK

Suddenly, after you die, those friends
who never agreed about anything
agree about your character.
They're like a houseful of singers rehearsing
the same score:
you were just, you were kind, you lived a fortunate life.
No harmony. No counterpoint. Except
they're not performers;
real tears are shed.

Luckily, you're dead; otherwise
you'd be overcome with revulsion.
But when that's passed,
when the guests begin filing out, wiping their eyes
because, after a day like this,
shut in with orthodoxy,
the sun's amazingly bright,
though it's late afternoon, September—
when the exodus begins,
that's when you'd feel
pangs of envy.

Your friends the living embrace one another,
gossip a little on the sidewalk
as the sun sinks, and the evening breeze
ruffles the women's shawls—
this, this, is the meaning of
"a fortunate life": it means
to exist in the present.

Request

LAWRENCE RAAB

For a long time I was sure
it should be "Jumping Jack Flash," then
the adagio from Schubert's C major Quintet,
but right now I want Oscar Peterson's

"You Look Good to Me." That's my request.
Play it at the end of the service,
after my friends have spoken.
I don't believe I'll be listening in,

but sitting here I'm imagining
you could be feeling what I'd like to feel—
defiance from the Stones, grief
and resignation with Schubert, but now

Peterson and Ray Brown are making
the moment sound like some kind
of release. Sad enough
at first, but doesn't it slide into

tapping your feet, then clapping
your hands, maybe standing up
in that shadowy hall in Paris
in the late sixties when this was recorded,

getting up and dancing
as I would not have done,
and being dead, cannot, but might
wish for you, who would then

understand what a poem—or perhaps only
the making of a poem, just that moment
when it starts, when so much
is still possible—

has allowed me to feel.
Happy to be there. Carried away.

Elegy

MEGHAN O'ROURKE

Flags breeze over tarmac in the club lot,
      container ships steam up the coast,

smokestacks like cigars
      between the loose lips of the bay.

Your nine iron drawn back for the swing,
      a half chuckle: that's where you left off,

in the surf of bees and grass
      at the twelfth hole, the remnants

of the host beneath your tongue,
      business card in pocket (Vice Pres., *American Shipping*).

Curiosity was your business.
      I ask you to come close.

Footsteps rustle in the witchgrass,
      cotton cuffs switch past, the stalks stir.

How lucky it is I was born
      to tell you the way it all turned out.

Translation

FRANZ WRIGHT

Death is nature's way
of telling you to be quiet.

Of saying it's time
to be weaned, your conflagration starved
to diamond.

I'll give you something to cry about.

And what those treetops swaying
dimly in the wind spelled.

Storm Valediction

CAMPBELL McGRATH

That sound is the thrashing of paper lanterns against the eaves.
Vessels frail as bodies lit with incandescent blood,
what else but that to survive the storm? What else could there be
to hold back the darkening rain of the city, empathy
like an opal, sorrow like a shriveled raisin
in the dust beneath the stove
but still a raisin. Pockets of odd coins, lint
to speak for transience and the rusted metal of fallen leaves,
paper cups with pastel scrimshaw elephants or diamonds, whatever
yolk the dawn subscribes for our delectation,
whatever throne the night sees fit to claim from the angels.
Difficult, difficult. All of it, any of it—
schoolgirls, vendors of sunglasses, businessmen
trembling their woes toward destiny and sleep—to feel it
or perish in the wicks of unlit candles,
to begin again within the inked shells of Easter eggs.
Steam is rising from grates, a child
pedals a bicycle through the alleyway of ghosts unafraid.
Purity, the maw of it, blackbirds and kestrels
against a sky the color of antique mah-jongg tiles, color of aspirin
dissolving in seawater as the sun bursts its amnion
of tattered clouds like the raw carcass of the heart revealed.
That sound is the ticking of paper lanterns in the storm.
Just that. It is hard
in the radiance of this world to live
but we live.

One Art

ELIZABETH BISHOP

The art of losing isn't hard to master;
so many things seem filled with the intent
to be lost that their loss is no disaster.

Lose something every day. Accept the fluster
of lost door keys, the hour badly spent.
The art of losing isn't hard to master.

Then practice losing farther, losing faster:
places, and names, and where it was you meant
to travel. None of these will bring disaster.

I lost my mother's watch. And look! my last, or
next-to-last, of three loved houses went.
The art of losing isn't hard to master.

I lost two cities, lovely ones. And, vaster,
some realms I owned, two rivers, a continent.
I miss them, but it wasn't a disaster.

—Even losing you (the joking voice, a gesture
I love) I shan't have lied. It's evident
the art of losing's not too hard to master
though it may look like (*Write* it!) like disaster.

Prayer

GALWAY KINNELL

Whatever happens. Whatever
what is is is what
I want. Only that. But that.

V.
Recovery

I learn by going where I have to go.
—THEODORE ROETHKE

My Heart

FRANK O'HARA

I'm not going to cry all the time
nor shall I laugh all the time,
I don't prefer one "strain" to another.
I'd have the immediacy of a bad movie,
not just a sleeper, but also the big,
overproduced first-run kind. I want to be
at least as alive as the vulgar. And if
some aficionado of my mess says "That's
not like Frank!", all to the good! I
don't wear brown and grey suits all the time,
do I? No. I wear workshirts to the opera,
often. I want my feet to be bare,
I want my face to be shaven, and my heart—
you can't plan on the heart, but
the better part of it, my poetry, is open.

Poem

SIMON ARMITAGE

Frank O'Hara was open on the desk
but I went straight for the directory.
Nick was out, Joey was engaged, Jim was
just making coffee and why didn't I

come over. I had Astrud Gilberto
singing "Bim Bom" on my Sony Walkman
and the sun was drying the damp slates on
the rooftops. I walked in without ringing

and he still wasn't dressed or shaved when we
topped up the coffee with his old man's Scotch
(it was only half ten but what the hell)
and took the newspapers into the porch.

Talking Heads were on the radio. I
was just about to mention the football
when he said "Look, will you help me clear her
wardrobe out?" I said "Sure Jim, anything."

The Gilded Shadow

JANE MAYHALL

The impact is simmering down, as into
a solvent liquid. That I'll never hear your voice
again, but through a medium like
rain. Or will see you but in a lightning flash.
You are nature's speech, the young girth
and deadly imprint.

I eagerly wait the date of your rebirth, in
the endless window-sky. Hovering cloud, really a
gilded shadow that lights your face outline. Waters
and land permit no elegy translated.
But a stark villanelle, facts rendered.
An indefinite, glorious seeding,

the element that draws us closest. Nucleus of
a meadow, the grass-tips' ghost your
being. Bend me to earth, the only hereafter after death.
O shades beneath the sun. Or I don't understand it—
like embracing a mystery hole in our minds,
this complex, heartbreak survival.

On New Terms

DEBORAH GARRISON

I'd like to begin again. Not touch my
own face, not tremble in the dark before
an intruder who never arrives. Not
apologize. Not scurry, not pace. Not
refuse to keep notes of what meant the most.
Not skirt my father's ghost. Not abandon
piano, or a book before the end.
Not count, count, count and wait, poised—the control,
the agony controlled—for the loss of
the one, having borne, I can't be, won't breathe
without: the foregone conclusion, the pain
not yet met, the preemptive mourning
without which
         nothing left of me but smoke.

For the Anniversary of My Death

W. S. MERWIN

Every year without knowing it I have passed the day
When the last fires will wave to me
And the silence will set out
Tireless traveller
Like the beam of a lightless star

Then I will no longer
Find myself in life as in a strange garment
Surprised at the earth
And the love of one woman
And the shamelessness of men
As today writing after three days of rain
Hearing the wren sing and the falling cease
And bowing not knowing to what

Hum

ANN LAUTERBACH

The days are beautiful.
The days are beautiful.

I know what days are.
The other is weather.

I know what weather is.
The days are beautiful.

Things are incidental.
Someone is weeping.

I weep for the incidental.
The days are beautiful.

Where is tomorrow?
Everyone will weep.

Tomorrow was yesterday.
The days are beautiful.

Tomorrow was yesterday.
Today is weather.

The sound of the weather
Is everyone weeping.

Everyone is incidental.
Everyone weeps.

The tears of today
Will put out tomorrow.

The rain is ashes.
The days are beautiful.

The rain falls down.
The sound is falling.

The sky is a cloud.
The days are beautiful.

The sky is dust.
The weather is yesterday.

The weather is yesterday.
The sound is weeping.

What is this dust?
The weather is nothing.

The days are beautiful.
The towers are yesterday.

The towers are incidental.
What are these ashes?

Here is the hate
That does not travel.

Here is the robe
That smells of the night

Here are the words
Retired to their books

Here are the stones
Loosed from their settings

Here is the bridge
Over the water

Here is the place
Where the sun came up

Here is a season
Dry in the fireplace.

Here are the ashes.
The days are beautiful.

Try to Praise the Mutilated World

ADAM ZAGAJEWSKI

Try to praise the mutilated world.
Remember June's long days,
and wild strawberries, drops of wine, the dew.
The nettles that methodically overgrow
the abandoned homesteads of exiles.
You must praise the mutilated world.
You watched the stylish yachts and ships;
one of them had a long trip ahead of it,
while salty oblivion awaited others.
You've seen the refugees heading nowhere,
you've heard the executioners sing joyfully.
You should praise the mutilated world.
Remember the moments when we were together
in a white room and the curtain fluttered.
Return in thought to the concert where music flared.
You gathered acorns in the park in autumn
and leaves eddied over the earth's scars.
Praise the mutilated world
and the gray feather a thrush lost,
and the gentle light that strays and vanishes
and returns.

Translated by Clare Cavanagh

Grief

MATTHEW DICKMAN

When grief comes to you as a purple gorilla
you must count yourself lucky.
You must offer her what's left
of your dinner, the book you were trying to finish
you must put aside
and make her a place to sit at the foot of your bed,
her eyes moving from the clock
to the television and back again.
I am not afraid. She has been here before
and now I can recognize her gait
as she approaches the house.
Some nights, when I know she's coming,
I unlock the door, lie down on my back,
and count her steps
from the street to the porch.
Tonight she brings a pencil and a ream of paper,
tells me to write down
everyone I have ever known
and we separate them between the living and the dead
so she can pick each name at random.
I play her favorite Willie Nelson album
because she misses Texas
but I don't ask why.
She hums a little,
the way my brother does when he gardens.
We sit for an hour
while she tells me how unreasonable I've been,
crying in the check-out line,

refusing to eat, refusing to shower,
all the smoking and all the drinking.
Eventually she puts one of her heavy
purple arms around me, leans
her head against mine,
and all of a sudden things are feeling romantic.
So I tell her,
things are feeling romantic.
She pulls another name, this time
from the dead
and turns to me in that way that parents do
so you feel embarrassed or ashamed of something.
Romantic? She says,
reading the name out loud, slowly
so I am aware of each syllable
wrapping around the bones like new muscle,
the sound of that person's body
and how reckless it is,
how careless that his name is in one pile and not the other.

My Father, in Heaven, Is Reading Out Loud

LI-YOUNG LEE

My father, in heaven, is reading out loud
to himself Psalms or news. Now he ponders what
he's read. No. He is listening for the sound
of children in the yard. Was that laughing
or crying? So much depends upon the
answer, for either he will go on reading,
or he'll run to save a child's day from grief.
As it is in heaven, so it was on earth.

Because my father walked the earth with a grave,
determined rhythm, my shoulders ached
from his gaze. Because my father's shoulders
ached from the pulling of oars, my life now moves
with a powerful back-and-forth rhythm:
nostalgia, speculation. Because he
made me recite a book a month, I forget
everything as soon as I read it. And knowledge
never comes but while I'm mid-stride a flight
of stairs, or lost a moment on some avenue.

A remarkable disappointment to him,
I am like anyone who arrives late
in the millennium and is unable
to stay to the end of days. The world's
beginnings are obscure to me, its outcomes
inaccessible. I don't understand
the source of starlight, or starlight's destinations.
And already another year slides out

of balance. But I don't disparage scholars;
my father was one and I loved him,
who packed his books once, and all of our belongings,
then sat down to await instruction
from his god, yes, but also from a radio.
At the doorway, I watched, and I suddenly
knew he was one like me, who got my learning
under a lintel; he was one of the powerless,
to whom knowledge came while he sat among
suitcases, boxes, old newspapers, string.

He did not decide peace or war, home or exile,
escape by land or escape by sea.
He waited merely, as always someone
waits, far, near, here, hereafter, to find out:
is it praise or lament hidden in the next moment?

Vigil

PHILLIS LEVIN

Why not wake at dawn? Why not break
From the coffin of night, whose nails
Are the only stars left. Why not follow
A tear like a comet's tail, and trail
The grief of a year until it ends—
Who knows where. Why not wake
At dawn, after all is gone, and go on?

Practice

ELLEN BRYANT VOIGT

To weep unbidden, to wake
at night in order to weep, to wait
for the whisker on the face of the clock
to twitch again, moving
the dumb day forward—

is this merely practice?
Some believe in heaven,
some in rest. *We'll float,*
you said. *Afterward*
we'll float between two worlds—

five bronze beetles
stacked like spoons in one
peony blossom, drugged by lust:
if I came back as a bird
I'd remember that—

until everyone we love
is safe is what you said.

Re: Happiness, in pursuit thereof

C. D. WRIGHT

It is 2005, just before landfall.
Here I am, a labyrinth, and I am a mess.
I am located at the corner of Waterway
and Bluff. I need your help. You will find me
to the left of the graveyard, where the trees
grow especially talkative at night,
where fog and alcohol rub off the edge.
We burn to make one another sing;
to stay the lake that it not boil, earth
not rock. We are running on Aztec time,
fifth and final cycle. Eyes switch on/off.
We would be mercurochrome to one another
bee balm or chamomile. We should be concrete,
glass, and spandex. We should be digital or,
at least, early. Be ivory-billed. Invisible
except to the most prepared observer.
We will be stardust. Ancient tailings
of nothing. Elapsed breath. No,
we must first be ice. Be nails. Be teeth.
Be lightning.

Light Turnouts

JOHN ASHBERY

Dear ghost, what shelter
in the noonday crowd? I'm going to write
an hour, then read
what someone else has written.

You've no mansion for this to happen in.
But your adventures are like safe houses,
your knowing where to stop an adventure
of another order, like seizing the weather.

We too are embroiled in this scene of happening,
and when we speak the same phrase together:
"We used to have one of those,"
it matters like a shot in the dark.

One of us stays behind.
One of us advances on the bridge
as on a carpet. Life—it's marvelous—
follows and falls behind.

Living Alone (II)

DENISE LEVERTOV

Some days, though,
living alone,
there's only knowledge of silence,
clutter of bells cobwebbed
in crumbling belfry,
words jaggéd,
in midutterance broken.

Starlings, as before,
whistle wondering at themselves,
crescendo, diminuendo.
My heart pounds away,
confident as a clock.
Yet there is silence.

New leafed, the neighbor trees
round out. There's one,
near my window,
seems to have no buds, though.

Beach Roses

MARK DOTY

What are they, the white roses,
when they are almost nothing,
only a little denser than the fog,

shadow-centered petals blurring,
toward the edges, into everything?

This morning one broken cloud
built an archipelago,
                        fourteen gleaming islands

hurrying across a blank plain of sheen:
nothing, or next to nothing

—pure scattering, light on light,
fleeting.
           And now, a heap of roses
beside the sea, white rugosa
beside the foaming hem of shore:
                        brave,

waxen candles . . .

                And we talk
as if death were a line to be crossed.
Look at them, the white roses.
Tell me where they end.

Death Poem

KIM ADDONIZIO

Do I have to bring it up again, isn't there another subject?
Can I forget about the scrap of flattened squirrel fur
fluttering on the road, can I forget the road
and how I can't stop driving no matter what,
not even for gas, or love, can I please not think
about my father left in some town behind me,
in his blue suit, with his folded hands,
and my grandmother moaning about her bladder
and swallowing all the pills, and the towns I'm passing now
can I try not to see them, the children squatting
by the ditches, the holes in their chests and foreheads,
the woman cradling her tumor, the dog dragging its crippled hips?
I can close my eyes and sit back if I want to,
I can lean against my friends' shoulders
and eat as they're eating, and drink from the bottle
being passed back and forth; I can lighten up, can't I,
Christ, can't I? There is another subject, in a minute
I'll think of it. I will. And if you know it, help me.
Help me. Remind me why I'm here.

Infirm

GWENDOLYN BROOKS

Everybody here
is infirm.
Everybody here is infirm.
Oh. Mend me. Mend me. Lord.

Today I
say to them
say to them
say to them, Lord:
look! I am beautiful, beautiful with
my wing that is wounded
my eye that is bonded
or my ear not funded
or my walk all a-wobble.
I'm enough to be beautiful.

You are
beautiful too.

It Is What It Is

PAUL MULDOON

It is what it is, the popping underfoot of the Bubble Wrap
in which Asher's new toy came,
popping like bladder wrack on the foreshore
of a country toward which I've been rowing
for fifty years, my peeping from behind a tamarind
at the peeping ox and ass, the flyer for a pantomime,
the inlaid cigarette box, the shamrock-painted jug,
the New Testament bound in red leather
lying open, Lordie, on her lap
while I mull over the rules of this imperspicuous game
that seems to be missing one piece, if not more.
Her voice at the gridiron coming and going
as if snatched by a sea wind.
My mother. Shipping out for good. For good this time.
The game. The plaything spread on the rug.
The fifty years I've spent trying to put it together.

12/19/02

DAVID LEHMAN

It seemed nothing would ever be the same
This feeling lasted for months
Not a day passed without a dozen mentions
of the devastation and the grief
Then life came back
it returned like sap to the tree
shooting new life into the veins
of parched leaves turning them green
and the old irritations came back,
they were life, too,
crowds pushing, taxis honking, the envies, the anger,
the woman who could not escape her misery
as she stood between two mirrored walls
couldn't sleep, took a pill, heard the noises of neighbors
the dogs barking, the pigeons in the alley yipping weirdly
and the phone that rang at eight twenty with the news
of Lucy's overdose we just saw her last Friday evening
at Jay's on Jane Street she'd been dead for a day or so
when they found her and there was no note
the autopsy's today the wake day after tomorrow
and then I knew that life had resumed, ordinary bitching life
had come back

Weeds and Peonies

DONALD HALL

Your peonies burst out, white as snow squalls,
with red flecks at their shaggy centers
in your border of prodigies by the porch.
I carry one magnanimous blossom indoors
and float it in a glass bowl, as you used to do.

Ordinary pleasures, contentment recollected,
blow like snow into the abandoned garden,
overcoming the daisies. Your blue coat
vanishes down Pond Road into imagined snowflakes
with Gus at your side, his great tail swinging,

but you will not reappear, tired and satisfied,
and grief's repeated particles suffuse the air—
like the dog yipping through the entire night,
or the cat stretching awake, then curling
as if to dream of her mother's milky nipples.

A raccoon dislodged a geranium from its pot.
Flowers, roots, and dirt lay upended
in the back garden where lilies begin
their daily excursions above stone walls
in the season of old roses. I pace beside weeds

and snowy peonies, staring at Mount Kearsarge
where you climbed wearing purple hiking boots.
"Hurry back. Be careful, climbing down."
Your peonies lean their vast heads westward
as if they might topple. Some topple.

The Lilacs

RICHARD WILBUR

Those laden lilacs
                at the lawn's end
Came stark, spindly,
                  and in staggered file,
Like walking wounded
                    from the dead of winter.
We watched them waken
                    in the brusque weather
To rot and rootbreak,
                to ripped branches,
And saw them shiver
                  as the memory swept them
Of night and numbness
                  and the taste of nothing.
Out of present pain
                and from past terror
Their bullet-shaped buds
                    came quick and bursting,
As if they aimed
              to be open with us!
But the sun suddenly
                settled about them,
And green and grateful
                the lilacs grew,
Healed in that hush,
             that hospital quiet
These lacquered leaves
              where the light paddles

And the big blooms

                        buzzing among them

Have kept their counsel,

                        conveying nothing

Of their mortal message,

                        unless one should measure

The depth and dumbness

                        of death's kingdom

By the pure power

                        of this perfume.

Father

TED KOOSER

May 19, 1999

Today you would be ninety-seven
if you had lived, and we would all be
miserable, you and your children,
driving from clinic to clinic,
an ancient, fearful hypochondriac
and his fretful son and daughter,
asking directions, trying to read
the complicated, fading map of cures.
But with your dignity intact
you have been gone for twenty years,
and I am glad for all of us, although
I miss you every day—the heartbeat
under your necktie, the hand cupped
on the back of my neck, Old Spice
in the air, your voice delighted with stories.
On this day each year you loved to relate
that at the moment of your birth
your mother glanced out the window
and saw lilacs in bloom. Well, today
lilacs are blooming in side yards
all over Iowa, still welcoming you.

After My Death

DAVID YOUNG

1

It will all go backward. Leaves
that fell in October will float up
and gather in trees for greening.
The fire I built will pull
its smoke back in while the logs
blaze and grow whole. Lost hailstones
will freeze themselves back into beads,
bounce once and rise up in a storm,
and as flowers unwilt and then tighten to buds
and the sun goes back to where it rose
I will step out through shrinking grass
at one for the first time
with my own breath, the wax
and wane of moon, dewsoak, tidewheel,
the kiss of puddle and star.

2

It will all go on. Rime frost, mist;
at the cracked mirror the janitor
will comb his hair and hum, three boys
will build a raft, chalk dust will settle
in blackboard troughs, trucks bump
on the railroad crossing, soft talk in trees,
a girl practicing her fiddle: I know this,
I keep imagining it, or trying, and sometimes
when I try hard, it is a small stone fern

delicate, changeless, heavy in my hand.
And then it weighs nothing
and then it is green
and everything is breathing.

Lucky Life

GERALD STERN

Lucky life isn't one long string of horrors
and there are moments of peace, and pleasure, as I lie in between
      the blows.
Lucky I don't have to wake up in Phillipsburg, New Jersey,
on the hill overlooking Union Square or the hill overlooking
Kuebler Brewery or the hill overlooking SS. Philip and James
but have my own hills and my own vistas to come back to.

Each year I go down to the island I add
one more year to the darkness;
and though I sit up with my dear friends
trying to separate the one year from the other,
this one from the last, that one from the former,
another from another,
after a while they all get lumped together,
the year we walked to Holgate,
the year our shoes got washed away,
the year it rained,
the year my tooth brought misery to us all.

This year was a crisis. I knew it when we pulled
the car onto the sand and looked for the key.
I knew it when we walked up the outside steps
and opened the hot icebox and began the struggle
with swollen drawers and I knew it when we laid out
the sheets and separated the clothes into piles
and I knew it when we made our first rush onto
the beach and I knew it when we finally sat
on the porch with coffee cups shaking in our hands.

My dream is I'm walking through Phillipsburg, New Jersey,
and I'm lost on South Main Street. I am trying to tell,
by memory, which statue of Christopher Columbus
I have to look for, the one with him slumped over
and lost in weariness or the one with him
vaguely guiding the way with a cross and globe in
one hand and a compass in the other.
My dream is I'm in the Eagle Hotel on Chamber Street
sitting at the oak bar, listening to two
obese veterans discussing Hawaii in 1942,
and reading the funny signs over the bottles.
My dream is I sleep upstairs over the honey locust
and sit on the side porch overlooking the stone culvert
with a whole new set of friends, mostly old and humorless.

Dear waves, what will you do for me this year?
Will you drown out my scream?
Will you let me rise through the fog?
Will you fill me with that old salt feeling?
Will you let me take my long steps in the cold sand?
Will you let me lie on the white bedspread and study
the black clouds with the blue holes in them?
Will you let me see the rusty trees and the old monoplanes one
          more year?
Will you still let me draw my sacred figures
and move the kites and the birds around with my dark mind?

Lucky life is like this. Lucky there is an ocean to come to.
Lucky you can judge yourself in this water.
Lucky you can be purified over and over again.
Lucky there is the same cleanliness for everyone.
Lucky life is like that. Lucky life. Oh lucky life.
Oh lucky lucky life. Lucky life.

Wait

GALWAY KINNELL

Wait, for now.
Distrust everything if you have to.
But trust the hours. Haven't they
carried you everywhere, up to now?
Personal events will become interesting again.
Hair will become interesting.
Pain will become interesting.
Buds that open out of season will become interesting.
Second-hand gloves will become lovely again;
their memories are what give them
the need for other hands. And the desolation
of lovers is the same: that enormous emptiness
carved out of such tiny beings as we are
asks to be filled; the need
for the new love *is* faithfulness to the old.

Wait.
Don't go too early.
You're tired. But everyone's tired.
But no one is tired enough.
Only wait a little and listen:
music of hair,
music of pain,
music of looms weaving all our loves again.
Be there to hear it, it will be the only time,
most of all to hear
the flute of your whole existence,
rehearsed by the sorrows, play itself into total exhaustion.

Wild Geese

MARY OLIVER

You do not have to be good.
You do not have to walk on your knees
for a hundred miles through the desert, repenting.
You only have to let the soft animal of your body
      love what it loves.
Tell me about despair, yours, and I will tell you mine.
Meanwhile the world goes on.
Meanwhile the sun and the clear pebbles of the rain
are moving across the landscapes,
over the prairies and the deep trees,
the mountains and the rivers.
Meanwhile the wild geese, high in the clean blue air,
are heading home again.
Whoever you are, no matter how lonely,
the world offers itself to your imagination,
calls to you like the wild geese, harsh and exciting—
over and over announcing your place
in the family of things.

The Waking

THEODORE ROETHKE

I wake to sleep, and take my waking slow.
I feel my fate in what I cannot fear.
I learn by going where I have to go.

We think by feeling. What is there to know?
I hear my being dance from ear to ear.
I wake to sleep, and take my waking slow.

Of those so close beside me, which are you?
God bless the Ground! I shall walk softly there,
And learn by going where I have to go.

Light takes the Tree; but who can tell us how?
The lowly worm climbs up a winding stair;
I wake to sleep, and take my waking slow.

Great Nature has another thing to do
To you and me; so take the lively air,
And, lovely, learn by going where to go.

This shaking keeps me steady. I should know.
What falls away is always. And is near.
I wake to sleep, and take my waking slow.
I learn by going where I have to go.

VI.
Redemption

What will survive of us is love.
—PHILIP LARKIN

The Trees

PHILIP LARKIN

The trees are coming into leaf
Like something almost being said;
The recent buds relax and spread,
Their greenness is a kind of grief.

Is it that they are born again
And we grow old? No, they die too.
Their yearly trick of looking new
Is written down in rings of grain.

Yet still the unresting castles thresh
In fullgrown thickness every May.
Last year is dead, they seem to say,
Begin afresh, afresh, afresh.

In the City of Light

LARRY LEVIS

The last thing my father did for me
Was map a way: he died, & so
Made death possible. If he could do it, I
Will also, someday, be so honored. Once,

At night, I walked through the lit streets
Of New York, from the Gramercy Park Hotel
Up Lexington & at that hour, alone,
I stopped hearing traffic, voices, the racket

Of spring wind lifting a newspaper high
Above the lights. The streets wet,
And shining. No sounds. Once,

When I saw my son be born, I thought
How loud this world must be to him, how final.

That night, out of respect for someone missing,
I stopped listening to it.

Out of respect for someone missing,
I have to say

This isn't the whole story.
The fact is, I was still in love.
My father died, & I was still in love. I know
It's in bad taste to say it quite this way. Tell me,
How *would* you say it?

The story goes: wanting to be alone & wanting
The easy loneliness of travelers,

I said good-bye in an airport & flew west.
It happened otherwise.
And where I'd held her close to me,
My skin felt raw, & flayed.

Descending, I looked down at light lacquering fields
Of pale vines, & small towns, each
With a water tower; then the shadows of wings;
Then nothing.

My only advice is not to go away.
Or, go away. Most

Of my decisions have been wrong.

When I wake, I lift cold water
To my face. I close my eyes.

A body wishes to be held, & held, & what
Can you do about that?

Because there are faces I might never see again,
There are two things I want to remember
About light, & what it does to us.

Her bright, green eyes at an airport—how they widened
As if in disbelief;
And my father opening the gate: a lit, & silent

City.

And Death Shall Have No Dominion

DYLAN THOMAS

And death shall have no dominion.
Dead men naked they shall be one
With the man in the wind and the west moon;
When their bones are picked clean and the clean bones gone,
They shall have stars at elbow and foot;
Though they go mad they shall be sane,
Though they sink through the sea they shall rise again;
Though lovers be lost love shall not;
And death shall have no dominion.

And death shall have no dominion.
Under the windings of the sea
They lying long shall not die windily;
Twisting on racks when sinews give way,
Strapped to a wheel, yet they shall not break;

Faith in their hands shall snap in two,
And the unicorn evils run them through;
Split all ends up they shan't crack:
And death shall have no dominion.

And death shall have no dominion.
No more may gulls cry at their ears
Or waves break loud on the seashores;
Where blew a flower may a flower no more
Lift its head to the blows of the rain;
Though they be mad and dead as nails
Heads of the characters hammer through daisies;
Break in the sun till the sun breaks down,
And death shall have no dominion.

What Are Years?

MARIANNE MOORE

What is our innocence,
what is our guilt? All are
    naked, none is safe. And whence
is courage: the unanswered question,
the resolute doubt,—
dumbly calling, deafly listening—that
in misfortune, even death,
        encourages others
        and in its defeat, stirs

    the soul to be strong? He
sees deep and is glad, who
    accedes to mortality
and in his imprisonment rises
upon himself as
the sea in a chasm, struggling to be
free and unable to be,
        in its surrendering
        finds its continuing.

    So he who strongly feels,
behaves. The very bird,
    grown taller as he sings, steels
his form straight up. Though he is captive,
his mighty singing
says, satisfaction is a lowly
thing, how pure a thing is joy.
        This is mortality,
        this is eternity.

First Psalm

ANNE SEXTON

Let there be a God as large as a sunlamp to laugh his heat at you.

Let there be an earth with a form like a jigsaw and let it fit for all of ye.

Let there be the darkness of a darkroom out of the deep. A worm
room.

Let there be a God who sees light at the end of a long thin pipe and lets
it in.

Let God divide them in half.

Let God share his Hoodsie.

Let the waters divide so that God may wash his face in first light.

Let there be pin holes in the sky in which God puts his little finger.

Let the stars be a heaven of jelly rolls and babies laughing.

Let the light be called Day so that men may grow corn or take busses.

Let there be on the second day dry land so that all men may dry their
toes with Cannon towels.

Let God call this earth and feel the grasses rise up like angel hair.

Let there be bananas, cucumbers, prunes, mangoes, beans, rice and
candy canes.

Let them seed and reseed.

Let there be seasons so that we may learn the architecture of the sky
with eagles, finches, flickers, seagulls.

Let there be seasons so that we may put on twelve coats and shovel
snow or take off our skins and bathe in the Caribbean.

Let there be seasons so the sky dogs will jump across the sun in
December.

Let there be seasons so that the eel may come out of her green cave.

Let there be seasons so that the raccoon may raise his blood level.

Let there be seasons so that the wind may be hoisted for an orange
leaf.

Let there be seasons so that the rain will bury many ships.

Let there be seasons so that the miracles will fill our drinking glass
with runny gold.

Let there be seasons so that our tongues will be rich in asparagus and
limes.

Let there be seasons so that our fires will not forsake us and turn to
metal.

Let there be seasons so that a man may close his palm on a woman's
breast and bring forth a sweet nipple, a starberry.

Let there be a heaven so that man may outlive his grasses.

Evening

CHARLES SIMIC

The snail gives off stillness.
The weed is blessed.
At the end of a long day
The man finds joy, the water peace.

Let all be simple. Let all stand still
Without a final direction.
That which brings you into the world
To take you away at death
Is one and the same;
The shadow long and pointy
Is its church.

At night some understand what the grass says.
The grass knows a word or two.
It is not much. It repeats the same word
Again and again, but not too loudly . . .

The Grasses

RUMI

The same wind that uproots trees
makes the grasses shine.

The lordly wind loves the weakness
and the lowness of grasses.
Never brag of being strong.

The axe doesn't worry how thick the branches are.
It cuts them to pieces. But not the leaves.
It leaves the leaves alone.

A flame doesn't consider the size of the woodpile.
A butcher doesn't run from a flock of sheep.

What is form in the presence of reality?
Very feeble. Reality keeps the sky turned over
like a cup above us, revolving. Who turns
the sky wheel? The universal intelligence.

And the motion of the body comes
from the spirit like a waterwheel
that's held in a stream.

The inhaling-exhaling is from spirit,
now angry, now peaceful.
Wind destroys, and wind protects.

There is no reality but God,
says the completely surrendered sheikh,
who is an ocean for all beings.

The levels of creation are straws in that ocean.
The movement of the straws comes from an agitation
in the water. When the ocean wants the straws calm,
it sends them close to shore. When it wants them
back in the deep surge, it does with them
as the wind does with the grasses.
                              This never ends.

Translated by Coleman Barks

Redemption Song

KEVIN YOUNG

Finally fall.
At last the mist,
heat's haze, we woke
these past weeks with

has lifted. We find
ourselves chill, a briskness
we hug ourselves in.
Frost greying the ground.

Grief might be easy
if there wasn't still
such beauty—would be far
simpler if the silver

maple didn't thrust
its leaves into flame,
trusting that spring
will find it again.

All this might be easier if
there wasn't a song
still lifting us above it,
if wind didn't trouble

my mind like water.
I half expect to see you
fill the autumn air
like breath—

At night I sleep
on clenched fists.
Days I'm like the child
who on the playground

falls, crying
not so much from pain
as surprise.
I'm tired of tide

taking you away,
then back again—
what's worse, the forgetting
or the thing

you can't forget.
Neither yet—
last summer's
choir of crickets

grown quiet.

from The Clay Hill Anthology

HAYDEN CARRUTH

Roads wear out slowly,
but they wear out. The milestones
twinkle in long grass.

. . .

Fathers die, but sons
catch the grave chill, looking in
at lost forgiveness.

. . .

Of course they prefer
hell to loneliness, of course
they go home to die.

. . .

For your love given
ask no return, none. To love
you must love to love.

. . .

Lover to lover
gasping *now*, and a star falls,
brightens, disappears.

. . .

Therefore to us, time's
final lesson: be content
with no monument.

• • •

Reaching again, spurned
again. Cat, you fill my hand
with masochism.

• • •

True, I happen. So
put "I" in. But randomly,
I am not the song.

• • •

Hear the night bellow,
our great black bull. Hear the dawn
distantly lowing.

• • •

Niobe, your tears
are your children now. See how
we have multiplied.

• • •

Let my snow-tracks lead
on, on. Let them, where they stop,
stop. There, in mid-field.

When Death Comes

MARY OLIVER

When death comes
like the hungry bear in autumn;
when death comes and takes all the bright coins from his purse

to buy me, and snaps the purse shut;
when death comes
like the measle-pox;

when death comes
like an iceberg between the shoulder blades,

I want to step through the door full of curiosity, wondering:
what is it going to be like, that cottage of darkness?

And therefore I look upon everything
as a brotherhood and a sisterhood,
and I look upon time as no more than an idea,
and I consider eternity as another possibility,

and I think of each life as a flower, as common
as a field daisy, and as singular,

and each name a comfortable music in the mouth,
tending, as all music does, toward silence,

and each body a lion of courage, and something
precious to the earth.

When it's over, I want to say: all my life
I was a bride married to amazement.
I was the bridegroom, taking the world into my arms.

When it's over, I don't want to wonder
if I have made of my life something particular, and real.
I don't want to find myself sighing and frightened,
or full of argument.

I don't want to end up simply having visited this world.

"i thank You God for most this amazing"
e. e. cummings

i thank You God for most this amazing
day:for the leaping greenly spirits of trees
and a blue true dream of sky;and for everything
which is natural which is infinite which is yes

(i who have died am alive again today,
and this is the sun's birthday; this is the birth
day of life and of love and wings:and of the gay
great happening illimitably earth)

how should tasting touching hearing seeing
breathing any—lifted from the no
of all nothing—human merely being
doubt unimaginable You?

(now the ears of my ears awake and
now the eyes of my eyes are opened)

Unsolicited Survey

PHILLIS LEVIN

Have you been there?

If so, can you describe the shape of the shadows?

When you entered, did anyone greet you?

Did the moss hug your foot or a jay screech in your ear?

Were you afraid you would not get back?

Did they ring a bell?

How many times, and what did it sound like?

Did a horse bow its head by the side of a road?

Did a single feather lie at the clearing?

Did a green wave cascade into a grove?

Did the flavor of light infect your sleep?

Did a toad leap from the dust onto a twig?

Did deer turn in terror as you passed?

Did a doe lick your hand and find you wanting?

Did you behold a flower that cannot fade?

Was the sky so empty that you fell upward?

Did the needles of a pine tickle your nose?

Did you sniff the ghost of the cedars of Lebanon?

Did you follow a petal blown to the edge of the sea?

Did you wake with a sheet twisted around your throat?

Did you call out?

Did you kneel at a blade of grass or the mound of an anthill?

Did you ask for a way in or a way out?

Did a bough sway imperceptibly?

Did you rest your hand on the shoulder of a god?

Did you open a piece of fruit and offer a portion of it to the sun?

How long did it take to finish, and were you satisfied?

Did a fly sip some water from a stone?

Did you touch the haze on a plum, its blue cloud?

Did you rub its skin until it lost its bloom?

Did the sun burn in a crow's eye?

Were the stars so clear another heaven appeared behind them?

Did you hear the wind consoling the leaves?

Did you look inside the cap of a mushroom, and part the curtain of
disbelief?

And Yet the Books

CZESLAW MILOSZ

And yet the books will be there on the shelves, separate beings,
That appeared once, still wet
As shining chestnuts under a tree in autumn,
And, touched, coddled, began to live
In spite of fires on the horizon, castles blown up,
Tribes on the march, planets in motion.
"We are," they said, even as their pages
Were being torn out, or a buzzing flame
Licked away their letters. So much more durable
Than we are, whose frail warmth
Cools down with memory, disperses, perishes.
I imagine the earth when I am no more:
Nothing happens, no loss, it's still a strange pageant,
Women's dresses, dewy lilacs, a song in the valley.
Yet the books will be there on the shelves, well born,
Derived from people, but also from radiance, heights.

Translated by Czeslaw Milosz and Robert Hass

Last Words

JAMES MERRILL

My life, your light green eyes
Have lit on me with joy.
There's nothing I don't know
Or shall not know again,
Over and over again.
It's noon, it's dawn, it's night,
I am the dog that dies
In the deep street of Troy
Tomorrow, long ago—
Part of me dims with pain,
Becomes the stinging flies,
The bent head of the boy.
Part looks into your light
And lives to tell you so.

Music Is in the Piano
Only When It Is Played

JACK GILBERT

We are not one with this world. We are not
the complexity our body is, nor the summer air
idling in the big maple without purpose.
We are a shape the wind makes in these leaves
as it passes through. We are not the wood
any more than the fire, but the heat which is a marriage
between the two. We are certainly not the lake
nor the fish in it, but the something that is
pleased by them. We are the stillness when
a mighty Mediterranean noon subtracts even the voices
of insects by the broken farmhouse. We are evident
when the orchestra plays, and yet are not part
of the strings or brass. Like the song that exists
only in the singing, and is not the singer.
God does not live among the church bells,
but is briefly resident there. We are occasional
like that. A lifetime of easy happiness mixed
with pain and loss, trying always to name and hold
on to the enterprise under way in our chest.
Reality is not what we marry as a feeling. It is what
walks up the dirt path, through the excessive heat
and giant sky, the sea stretching away.
He continues past the nunnery to the old villa
where he will sit on the terrace with her, their sides
touching. In the quiet that is the music of that place,
which is the difference between silence and windlessness.

Coda

JASON SHINDER

And now I know what most deeply connects us

after that summer so many years ago,
and it isn't poetry, although it is poetry,

and it isn't illness, although we have that in common,

and it isn't gratitude for every moment,
even the terrifying ones, even the physical pain,

though we are grateful, and it isn't even death,

though we are halfway through
it, or even the way you describe the magnificence

of being alive, catching a glimpse,

in the store window, of your blowing hair and chapped lips,
though it is beautiful, it is; but it is

that you're my friend out here on the far reaches

of what humans can find out about each other.

Litany

ARACELIS GIRMAY

when we are old & our hearts have beat within us, let
us go back, & when we have buried our loves, & shed
our bodies piece by piece, & when we have danced
& broken our shoes, & danced, let us go back,
when we have gone mad, & when we have shut
the doors, dismantled our eyes & rifles, let us go back,
when we have drunk the wine & licked our lips
& put our tongues to the inside of the green glass bottle
& laid down our bodies old as trees, streets, let us go back,
when we have told our stories & forgotten our stories,
& set the tables & made the beds, let us go back,
& received other bodies into our bodies, let us go,
when we have entered, & opened,
& opened our mouths, let us go back,
& when we have crossed rivers on the back of a horse,
& read the palms & burned the candles,
& touched the cactus, & eaten the fruit, let us go back,
when we have tasted the salt, & our knees have touched
the ground, let us go back, when we have painted
our hands, let us go back, & when our hands
have touched the backs of other hands, let us go back,
& when we are old & nearly crossed over,
& all of our bones have walked within us,
& when we have planted flowers
& talked into the ears of our dogs, let us go back,
& when we have lost our mothers,
& sent our brothers away
& heard no news,

& when we have watched the rain from trains,
let us go back,
& when we have been moved by this & by that,
& sung the songs & disobeyed, & when we have turned
& turned & turned & turned, let us go back,
when we have boiled the tea, & tasted the bread,
& washed our right hands & walked through mountains,
when we have learned the children's names, let us go back,
& seen our reflections in the hyena's eye,
& walked under the ladders, & lit the frankincense,
& when we have seen the wars, let us go back,
& when we have given our fathers & gotten them back,
& when we have given our fathers & not gotten them back,
& when we have studied the maps & learned the languages,
& prayed over the food, let us go back,
when we have whispered the secrets, let us go back,
& when we have walked & calloused our heels,
let us go back, when we have braided the heads
& set the peppers out to dry, & laughed
& laughed & laughed & laughed, let us go back,
& when we have watched the stars & seen
the black-lined eyes of pirates selling beads,
let us go back, when we have tasted sweetnesses,
let us go back, when we have sewed the dresses
& licked the thread, let us go,
& when we have wanted water, let us go back,
when the poem has been sung,
when the strings & tambourines,
when all the birds have gathered at the window, let us go,
let us go back there, let us go back

Notes from the Other Side

JANE KENYON

I divested myself of despair
and fear when I came here.

Now there is no more catching
one's own eye in the mirror,

there are no bad books, no plastic,
no insurance premiums, and of course

no illness. Contrition
does not exist, nor gnashing

of teeth. No one howls as the first
clod of earth hits the casket.

The poor we no longer have with us.
Our calm hearts strike only the hour,

and God, as promised, proves
to be mercy clothed in light.

Self-Portrait

CHARLES WRIGHT

Someday they'll find me out, and my lavish hands,
Full moon at my back, fog groping the gone horizon, the edge
Of the continent scored in yellow, expectant lights,
White shoulders of surf, a wolf-colored sand,
The ashes and bits of char that will clear my name.

Till then, I'll hum to myself and settle the whereabouts.
Jade plants and oleander float in a shine.
The leaves of the pepper tree turn green.
My features are sketched with black ink in a slow drag through the sky,
Waiting to be filled in.

Hand that lifted me once, lift me again,
Sort me and flesh me out, fix my eyes.
From the mulch and the undergrowth, protect me and pass me on.
From my own words and my certainties,
From the rose and the easy cheek, deliver me, pass me on.

The Mother

ANNE STEVENSON

Of course I love them, they are my children.
That is my daughter and this my son.
And this is my life I give them to please them.
It has never been used. Keep it safe, pass it on.

Did This Ever Happen to You

FRANZ WRIGHT

A marble-colored cloud
engulfed the sun and stalled,

a skinny squirrel limped toward me
as I crossed the empty park

and froze, the last
or next to last

fall leaf fell but before it touched
the earth, with shocking clarity

I heard my mother's voice
pronounce my name. And in an instant I passed

beyond sorrow and terror, and was carried up
into the imageless

bright darkness
I came from

and am. Nobody's
stronger than forgiveness.

An Arundel Tomb

PHILIP LARKIN

Side by side, their faces blurred,
The earl and countess lie in stone,
Their proper habits vaguely shown
As jointed armour, stiffened pleat,
And that faint hint of the absurd—
The little dogs under their feet.

Such plainness of the pre-baroque
Hardly involves the eye, until
It meets his left-hand gauntlet, still
Clasped empty in the other; and
One sees, with a sharp tender shock,
His hand withdrawn, holding her hand.

They would not think to lie so long.
Such faithfulness in effigy
Was just a detail friends would see:
A sculptor's sweet commissioned grace
Thrown off in helping to prolong
The Latin names around the base.

They would not guess how early in
Their supine stationary voyage
The air would change to soundless damage,
Turn the old tenantry away;
How soon succeeding eyes begin
To look, not read. Rigidly they

Persisted, linked, through lengths and breadths
Of time. Snow fell, undated. Light
Each summer thronged the glass. A bright
Litter of birdcalls strewed the same
Bone-riddled ground. And up the paths
The endless altered people came,

Washing at their identity.
Now, helpless in the hollow of
An unarmorial age, a trough
Of smoke in slow suspended skeins
Above their scrap of history,
Only an attitude remains:

Time has transfigured them into
Untruth. The stone fidelity
They hardly meant has come to be
Their final blazon, and to prove
Our almost-instinct almost true:
What will survive of us is love.

Poem for a Survivor

DONALD JUSTICE

for R.G.S.

Holding this poem
Close, like a mirror,
I breathe upon it.

I watch for some sign.
There is a faint mist
Spreading across it.

It takes hold. It clings
To the lean hollows
As the sun rises,

This sun that is going
To burn the mist off.

I give you chamois
To clear the surface.

I give you this sun.

Letter from God

RUTH L. SCHWARTZ

I wanted to give you the swallow's egg, but it shattered,
Leaking yolk like joy. I wanted to give you the dead fish
But a bird had already stolen its eye. I wanted to give you the
      ruby socket
But the fish held tight. I wanted to give you the beach with its miles
Of brownish sand, mounds of bleached and broken shell,
But I changed my mind. I wanted to give you the trees with a little
Butter and lemon squeezed on top, but they were firmly planted.
I wanted to give you the slimy moss, the gnats like tiny exploding
      stars,
The driftwood crossed like mothers' arms. I wanted to give you
My hands, the morning bodies of dolphins,
Arcing easily from water, plunging in again. Hunger
And the absence of hunger. The willow trees bent low to the water,
The nippled peaks of the water, the living stone,
The names and hearts chiseled into the stone. Lovers say they will love
      forever
And in some other world, they might. In this world, a man on the
      boardwalk
Can write the entire Lord's Prayer on a grain of rice,
But everyone goes on running and dying
Like dogs on the beach, their bodies extended
Into forever, for nothing, for joy, for a stick.
I wanted to let you go but I thought I would die.
I wanted to let you live but you were already gone.
I wanted to sip you like fine wine, wanted to gut you like a trout,
Dip your delicate dripping spine
Like a holy feather into my mouth. I wanted South,

North, East and West. Wanted to praise you and catch you and
     throw you
Back, like one too small or one too beautiful
To keep. I wanted to marry you like the light
And then forget you like the dark. I wanted to promise you something,
     then give you
A thousand times what I'd promised, then take it away,
Then give it back again. There are sticks muscled as snakes,
Sticks never fetched, hopeless sticks. There are faithful sticks, and
     faithful
Mouths which carry them. There is a moon thin as Communion
Waiting to be dissolved on the tongue. There is a bluejay
In the tree, its feathers more dazzling than your veins,
There is a cardinal redder and brighter
Than your blood. Tongue of water, lip of water
Where two swallows mate like ribbons
Twisted into air.
This is it. Take it or leave it. Love,

Otherwise

JANE KENYON

I got out of bed
on two strong legs.
It might have been
otherwise. I ate
cereal, sweet
milk, ripe, flawless
peach. It might
have been otherwise.
I took the dog uphill
to the birch wood.
All morning I did
the work I love.

At noon I lay down
with my mate. It might
have been otherwise.
We ate dinner together
at a table with silver
candlesticks. It might
have been otherwise.
I slept in a bed
in a room with paintings
on the walls, and
planned another day
just like this day.
But one day, I know,
it will be otherwise.

To Breath

KENNETH KOCH

There is that in me—you come Sunday morning to entertain my life
With your existence. I am born and my mother warms me
She warms me with her self while you circulate through me
And fill me with air! My mother is so young
To have to deal with an entire existence, mine, apart from hers!
She needs you to replenish what's there—
Gala you, who stretch the seams.
Without you, the millions of joys of life would be nothing,
Only darkness, no pages in the book. In love you're there quickly
In the race through the forest, in the dangerous dive from the rock.
I have often sensed you at parties
The girls come up to the boys and all of them breathe
You're awake for them even while they sleep.
What I want you to do for me is this:
I want to understand certain things and tell them to others.
To do it, I have to get them right, so they are hard to resist.
Stay with me until I can do this.

Afterwards, you can go where you want.

Train Ride

RUTH STONE

All things come to an end;
small calves in Arkansas,
the bend of the muddy river.
Do all things come to an end?
No, they go on forever.
They go on forever, the swamp,
the vine-choked cypress, the oaks
rattling last year's leaves,
the thump of the rails, the kite,
the still white stilted heron.
All things come to an end.
The red clay bank, the spread hawk,
the bodies riding this train,
the stalled truck, pale sunlight, the talk;
the talk goes on forever,
the wide dry field of geese,
a man stopped near his porch
to watch. Release, release;
between cold death and a fever,
send what you will, I will listen.
All things come to an end.
No, they go on forever.

ACKNOWLEDGMENTS

Thanks to all those who made this book possible: especially to my agent Rob McQuilkin, who first suggested this book; to Kathy Belden for her editing expertise and continual support; to Laura Norman, my researcher, who helped with permissions, spreadsheets, and good humor. Thanks also to my family for support, both in putting together this book and in grief.

INDEX BY SUBJECT

This index lists poems by their subjects for those who would like to read in a more directed fashion. While any of the selections might serve for a funeral service, the first section includes poems frequently used in that way and ones especially well suited for reading aloud or for comfort.

FOR A FUNERAL SERVICE

MOTHERS

FATHERS

SPOUSES AND LOVERS

SIBLINGS

DAUGHTERS AND SONS

GRANDPARENTS AND ANCESTORS

FRIENDS AND STRANGERS

A NOTE ON THE EDITOR

KEVIN YOUNG is the author of six books of poetry, most recently *Dear Darkness*, named one of 2008's best "Books from Our Pages" by the *New Yorker*, and winner of a 2009 Southern Independent Booksellers Alliance Award; and *For the Confederate Dead*, winner of the Quill Award in Poetry and the Paterson Poetry Prize for Sustained Literary Achievement. His book *Jelly Roll: A Blues* was a finalist for both the National Book Award and the Los Angeles Times Book Prize and won the Paterson Poetry Prize. He is the editor of four other volumes, including *Blues Poems*, *Jazz Poems*, and the Library of America's *John Berryman: Selected Poems*. The curator of literary collections and the Raymond Danowski Poetry Library and Atticus Haygood Professor of English and Creative Writing at Emory University, Young lives in Boston and Atlanta.